JEWELLERY

20TH CENTURY

20TH CENTURY JEWELLERY

CAROLINE
PULLÉE

Grange
BOOKS

A QUANTUM BOOK

Published by Grange Books
An imprint of Grange Books plc
The Grange
Grange Yard
London SE1 3AG

ISBN 1-84013-028-8

QUMTCJ

Printed in Singapore by Star Standard Industries Pte Ltd

CONTENTS

INTRODUCTION 7

1

ART NOUVEAU AND AFTER 11
1895 – 1918

2

ART DECO 27
1919 – 1930

3

THE TWENTIES AND THIRTIES 39

4

THE SECOND WORLD WAR AND AFTER 51
1939 – 1949

5

THE GROWTH OF POPULAR CULTURE 65
1950 – 1965

6

CRAFTSMANSHIP VERSUS AESTHETICS: 77
THE MULTI-MEDIA FORM
AND FUNCTION OF JEWELRY DESIGN
1965 – 1990

Susan Barr shows a fluency of form and a use of colour more usually associated with two-dimensional art. *Long Tail* brooches, England, 1980s.

Introduction

DURING THE TWENTIETH CENTURY there has been a fundamental change in attitude towards jewelry in terms both of its design and its function. Increasing importance has been attached to the aesthetic merits of form, colour and texture rather than to the obvious financial value of the materials used.

The modern experiments with new, often synthetic materials and iconography, have resulted in some very powerful, occasionally eccentric designs. Although the traditional jewelry trade has continued to favour the use of precious gem stones and metals, it too has begun to search for a greater individuality in design.

Until the early twentieth century mainly precious or semi-precious materials were employed in the jewelry trade. Jewelry therefore continued to be the prerogative of the rich, and its role was to exhibit a person's position in society. The women who wore it were in effect walking bank statements, ambassadors of their husbands' social and economic stature. Until the eve of the First World War jewelry was always seen in this light, and of course for many it remains either a status symbol or a secure form of investment. For this market the well-established jewelry houses such as Boucheron, Asprey, Cartier and Fabergé continue to produce traditional jewelry forms. However, alongside them, there is now a buoyant and increasing interest in the creative individuality of the artist-jeweler, who caters for a much broader market. This area of jewelry design is not only generally more affordable, but is also quicker to respond to changing artistic trends and fashions. Together with the advent of cheap costume jewelry, this development represents the completely new attitude towards body ornamentation that has come about during the course of the twentieth century.

One of the factors that has brought about this revolution in jewelry design has been the maturing of industrialization and the growth of new technologies, enabling jewelry to be mass-produced. While this

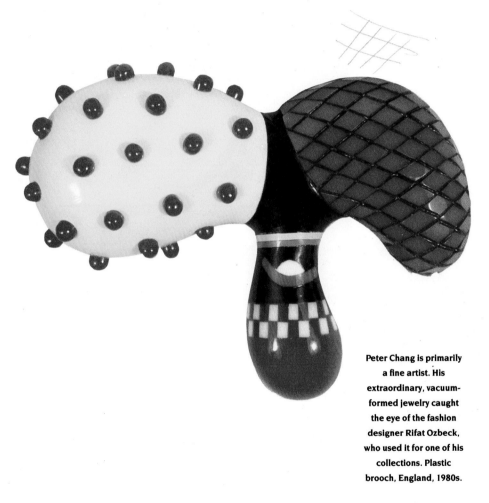

Peter Chang is primarily a fine artist. His extraordinary, vacuum-formed jewelry caught the eye of the fashion designer Rifat Ozbeck, who used it for one of his collections. Plastic brooch, England, 1980s.

David Watkins' eminence and influence as a pioneering artist/jeweler was justly recognized when he was invited to become Professor of the Jewelry and Metalwork Department at the Royal College of Art, London, in the mid-eighties. Torus 280 (BI) neckpiece, England, 1989.

has broadened the market to a less wealthy sector of society, it has also inevitably had enormous implications for design, some of which have been a cause for concern.

When factory production started in earnest in the mid-nineteenth century, many entrepreneurs and industrialists, in order to satisfy a growing consumer market, turned towards the indiscriminate use of ornamentation. Even the most mundane and utilitarian of machine-made goods, especially domestic appliances, were embellished to make them more attractive to the consumer. This was not a philanthropic exercise, indeed it was often done to conceal poor workmanship.

Individuals such as John Ruskin and William Morris were led to question the effects on art and design of large-scale production. The Arts and Crafts movement (begun in the 1860s) was a group of people interested in reinstating the aesthetic values of the artist/craftsman in place of those of

industrial production. Active members of this movement revealed evidence to suggest a general decline in manufactured design, and they drew attention to the serious implications this had for the decorative arts. The Arts and Crafts movement may have failed to change the path of commercial opportunism, but it did succeed in bringing about a new perception of design. The movement showed in particular how ideas and motifs from the past could be reinterpreted in modern ways. (They themselves were drawn, especially, to imagery from medieval humanism.) Since that period the criteria used to judge good design have been based on such factors as performance, aesthetic appeal and relationship to the environment.

Besides industrialization, a second major influence on jewelry and other design in the twentieth century has been the rapid expansion of information technology and the media. New ideas can now be propagated not only nationwide but worldwide, more efficiently than ever before. People are better informed, and are involved with international, as well as national, affairs. Inevitably, this change in public perception has brought with it a need for a modern aesthetic, which is clearly reflected in the recent history of jewelry design. There is now a far greater choice of exciting new ideas and markets which reflect the taste and aspirations of a multi-cultural society.

The third major factor that has led to the huge changes in jewelry design of this century has been the way that society itself has changed in the West. From the end of the nineteenth century to the present there has been a marked decline in the aristocracy and an ever increasing growth in the middle classes. This has meant that, whereas the market for jewelry before this century was exclusive to the privileged classes, now there is a huge new market of people able to spend money on luxury items such as jewelry, particularly when it is available at reasonable prices.

All these factors have combined to make the twentieth century a period of revolution in jewelry design, and the history of how jewelry has changed reflects much of the social history of our times.

Wendy Ramshaw's route from fashion design to jewelry in the late sixties might account for her continuing ability to produce new and challenging work which nevertheless retains an accessible appeal. Neckpiece, England, 1980s.

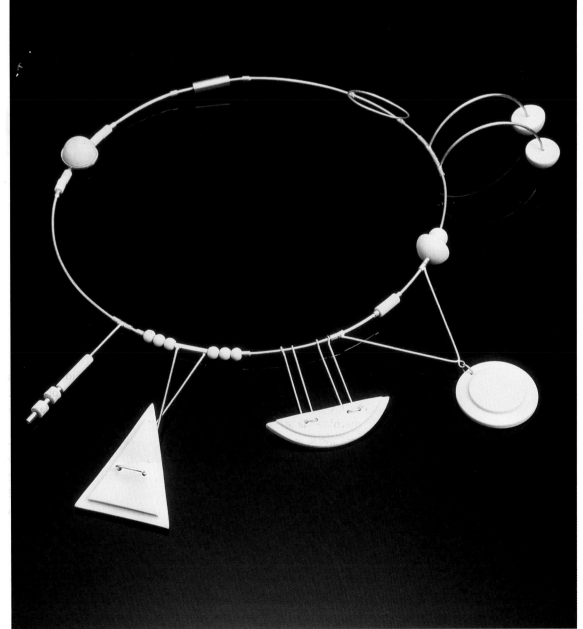

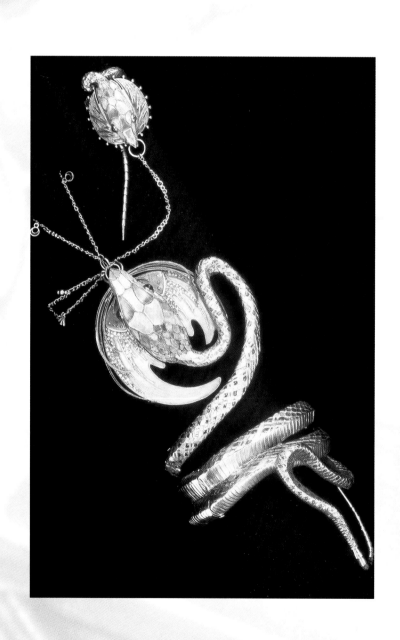

ONE

Art Nouveau and After

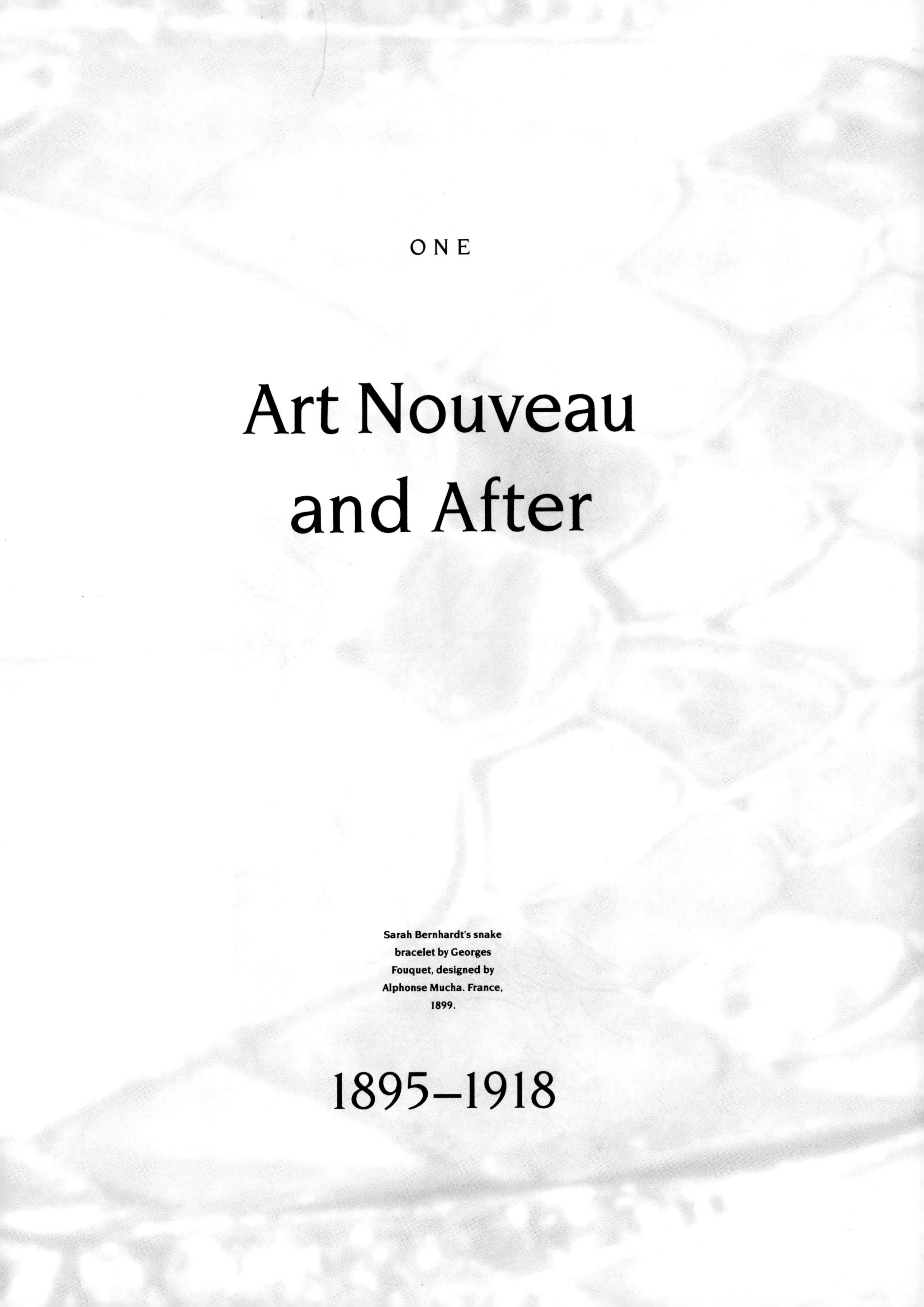

Sarah Bernhardt's snake
bracelet by Georges
Fouquet, designed by
Alphonse Mucha. France,
1899.

1895–1918

ART NOUVEAU, MEANING 'NEW art', seems an apt description for an art movement that bridged the psychological gap between the old and the new centuries. As the 1900s dawned, the historicism inspired by the Arts and Crafts movement began giving way to a new forward-looking approach, and a search for a truly modern style. Art Nouveau, which spanned the period 1895 to 1905, is caught between the joint influences of the old and new ideas, and owes something to each of them.

One of the major influences on Art Nouveau was the Symbolist movement, which had begun in the 1880s. The imagery adopted by this group of artists combined religious mysticism with eroticism, as seen particularly in the work of the Austrian painter, Gustav Klimt. Art Nouveau combined inspiration from this source with some of the elements of Arts and Crafts philosophy. In its highly varied and asymmetrical forms, it also reflected the political uneasiness of its period.

Art Nouveau concentrated on the rich treatment of surface decoration. It was a style that was applied to everything from fine art to architecture and interior design. Hector Guimard's Paris Metro station, for instance, was Art Nouveau in style, as were the interior designs of the Belgian architect, Victor Horta, with their curvilinear decoration.

Most characteristic of Art Nouveau is a tendency to asymmetry, producing a sense of instability which is highlighted through the use of whiplash curves and tendrils. Another ubiquitous presence is the *femme fatale* – the seductive nymph of Pre-Raphaelite paintings. Much of the imagery in Art Nouveau comes from mythology, whether in the form of winged dragons and serpents (portents of evil), the gothic horrors of vampires and bats or more ethereal creatures such as the peacock and the dragonfly.

In jewelry design, the Art Nouveau style led to a move away from precious stones and towards non-precious compositions, particularly in bronze, glass, mother-of-pearl and ivory.

Detail of a wrought iron staircase from the Hotel Solvay, Brussels, 1895–1900, designed by Belgian architect and designer Victor Horta.

— ◆ —

Lalique and the beginning of Art Nouveau jewelry

Art Nouveau jewelry had its origins in the work of French goldsmiths, whose creations were the inspiration for other European craftsmen and women. Most influential among the French artist-jewelers was the glass-maker René Lalique. He had a profound impact throughout Europe and America, starting when he opened a shop in Paris in 1885. He showed his work at the Salon du Champ Mars gallery in 1895 and again at the Paris exhibition of 1900. He has become particularly renowned for the pieces he made for the actress Sarah Bernhardt. They were a bold and extravagant celebration of mythology, combining engraved and stained glass in a theatrical style appropriate to the world of the actress.

Lalique linked precious materials with lesser ones such as horn, using a wide variety of techniques, including casting and *plique-à-jour*. By using many different materials he was able to match the colour of a piece of jewelry to a dress design. He used gold enamels, large pearls and a galaxy of semi-precious stones to create glowing, exuberant jewelry that was distinctively his own.

Other important names in the field included Georges Fouquet who commissioned Alphonse Mucha, a Czech painter and graphic artist, to design more jewelry for Bernhardt. On the whole, his designs were more synthetic and geometric than Lalique's. Lucien Gaillard, Eugène Feuillâtre and Henri and Paul Vever of *La Maison Vever* were other major figures of the time, as was Edward Colonna. The latter designed furniture for Samuel Bing's *La Maison de l'Art Nouveau*, the shop that gave its name to this movement.

The new art jewelry being produced by these designers excited much debate as to its wearability, not least because the pieces were generally very large. Many of the designers also made more commercial jewelry that had wider popular appeal whilst retaining the same aesthetic qualities as the art pieces.

Jewelers in France in this period had to produce ever more lavish and exuberant pieces for a society that was celebrating the final years of *La Belle Epoque*. Their work is symbolic, figurative and ostentatious, taking its inspiration from sources as wide-ranging as imported Japanese designs, Symbolism and ecclesiastical imagery.

Art Nouveau styles were adopted not only by the artist-jewelers, but also by the well-established companies centred in Paris such as Cartier and Boucheron, and by retailers like Julius Meier-Graef's *La Maison Moderne*, which sold designs by Paul Follot and Maurice Dufrêne.

—·◆·—

Art Nouveau jewelry
in Britain

Jewelry in Britain at the turn of the century differed from the French because it was more backward-looking and still owed much to the Arts and Crafts. The British decorative motifs featured primeval figures and floral tributes combined with interlace patterns of Celtic origin. These pieces were made in finely crafted silver enriched with polished stones and enamels. They took the form of belt or waist buckles, clasps, hatpins and pendants, reminiscent of the trappings of civic functions. Designers included Archibald Knox, Oliver Baker, Jessie King, Kate Fischer and John Paul

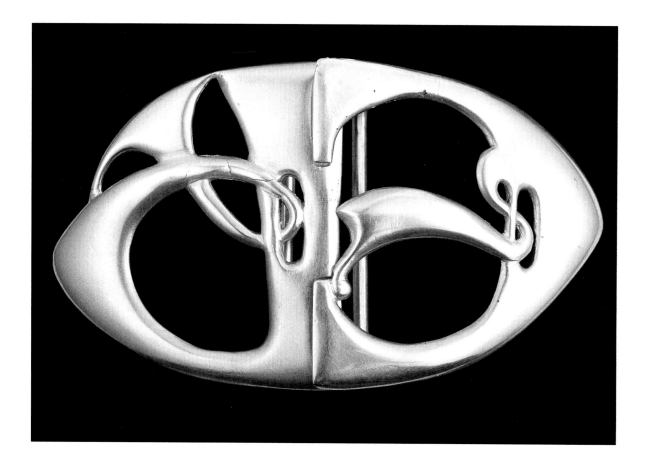

Silver belt buckle designed by Archibald Knox, who worked for Liberty & Co in the first decade of the 20th century. It has a stylized, abstract quality, similar to the more asymmetric design of European Art Nouveau. England, 1905.

An architect who set up
the Guild of Handicraft,
C R Ashbee's work
reflects the reaction to
the heavy court jewelry of
the time. In the tradition
of the Arts and Crafts
movement, he used
birds, flowers and
natural forms in light
colours – silver and pale
blues. Pendant, England,
c 1900.

An enamelled silver buckle decorated with a floral motif by the Arts and Crafts jeweler Nelson Dawson, who was a founder of the Artificers' Guild, Britain, early 1900s.

Cooper. Many of these were employed by Liberty, a shop established in 1875 which specialized in Oriental goods from the East Indies and Japan. Liberty maintained a strict policy of anonymity regarding the designers it commissioned to make jewelry. However it is possible to identify the work of many of these jewelers since they were also prominent in their own right as members of the Arts and Crafts movement.

A number of guilds were also established in Britain at the turn of the century. These were medieval-style associations of craftsmen concerned to protect their traditional trade practices. The Guild School of Handicraft was set up by architect and jeweler CR Ashbee in 1888, and included designers such as Fred Partridge and May Hart. The Artificers' Guild was founded three years later by Nelson Dawson. The members of these guilds worked in a number of different media, exploring the properties of horn and shell, cloissoné and *plique-à-jour* enamelling.

Other British jewelry designers of the time included Sybil Dunlop, Arthur and Georgina Gaskin, Henry Wilson, Harold Stabler and Omar Ramsden. Their work drew inspiration from the religious iconography of the Renaissance, from medievalism and Scandinavian folk art.

Probably the most significant contribution to British Art Nouveau was the work produced by the Glasgow School of Art, led by the architect and designer, Charles Rennie Mackintosh. He incorporated the essence of Art Nouveau's curvilinear forms with traditional Celtic motifs.

Earrings, brooch and
pendant by Sybil Dunlop,
a Scottish jeweler based
in London. Sybil Dunlop's
work is reminiscent of
earlier English Arts and
Crafts jewelry from the
turn of the century, with
its fine delicate gem set
pieces which can be seen
in this collection. Britain,
1920s.

America and Tiffany

Until the first decade of the twentieth century most American jewelry was imported from European collections. The first large-scale home production began at the turn of the century when corporations such as Gorham, Rhode Island, and Krementz, New Jersey started to manufacture Gallic imitations. The most outstanding and prestigious jewelry establishment in America at this time was Tiffany and Co. This company had been founded in 1834, under the directorship of Louis Comfort Tiffany, a painter who had studied in Paris. The company became involved in all branches of the decorative arts, including wrought iron and stained glass. In 1902 Tiffanys opened an art jewelry department, which concentrated on the sort of Byzantine and Oriental pieces that were being promoted by its English counterpart, Liberty and Co. This was unusual at the time in America, where most other available jewelry designs were based on Gallic Art Nouveau. Tiffany began to experiment with new combinations of colours and materials and were the first to make jewelry out of Lava glass.

— · ◆ · —

The *Jugend* magazine, a German journal established in 1896 which not only supported the Art Nouveau movement but also provided an opportunity for artists to show their work nationwide.

'Jugendstijl' in Germany

In Germany, the equivalent of Art Nouveau was known as Jugendstijl, which became a major influence on the decorative arts by 1900. In 1907, the Deutscher Werkbund was formed to promote an alliance between art and industry. It was a teaching institution started by Henry van der Velde and Hermann Muthesius, partially inspired by British design developments. Its influence is particularly evident in the mass-produced jewelry designs of the company of Theodor Fahrner in Pforzheim, which was the centre of the German jewelry industry between 1900 and 1930.

The Deutscher Werkbund was interested not only in applying good design principles, but also in educating the general public to appreciate these principles. Their ultimate goal was to help shape the economic and cultural identity of modern Germany. As well as Henry van der Velde, designers from the Deutscher Werkbund included Josef Maria Olbrich and Patriz Huber, together with a colony of artists in Darmstadt who were allied to the British Arts and Crafts movement.

— · ◆ · —

ABOVE
—
A rather formalized, symmetrical composition can be seen in these brooches, which contrasts with the more organic and flowing lines of Gallic Art Nouveau. A typical example of European Art Nouveau jewelry, c 1905.

LEFT
—
Silver and amethyst necklace manufactured in 1905 by the firm Theodor Fahrner in Pforzheim, the centre of the German jewelry industry, and inspired by the rectalinear qualities of Art Nouveau.

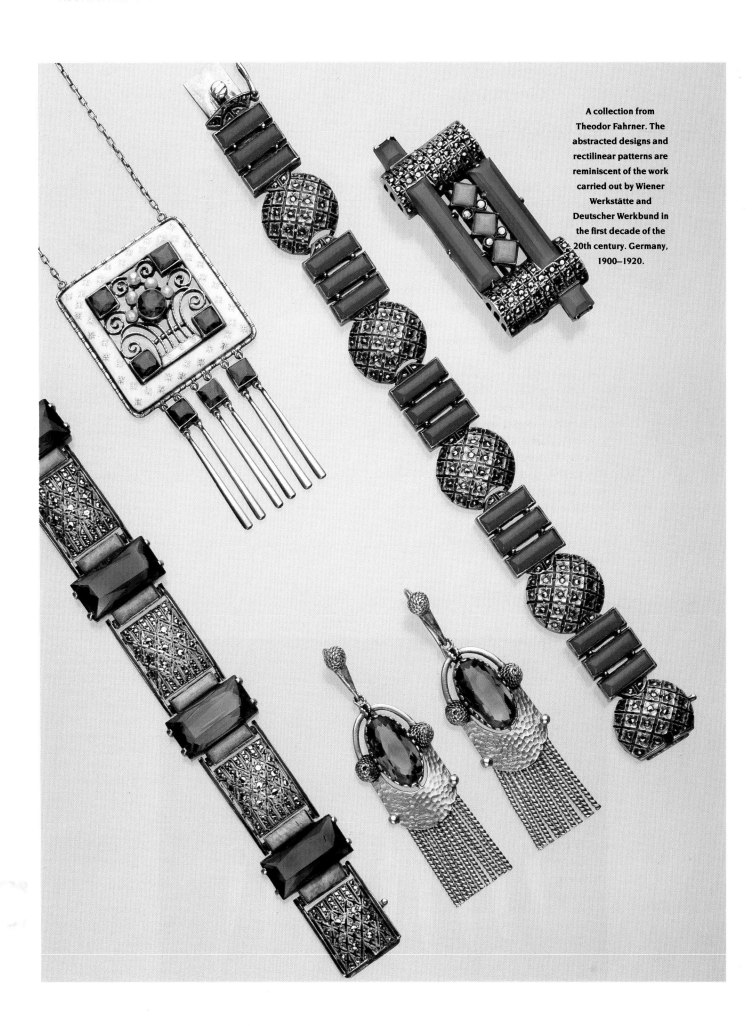

A collection from Theodor Fahrner. The abstracted designs and rectilinear patterns are reminiscent of the work carried out by Wiener Werkstätte and Deutscher Werkbund in the first decade of the 20th century. Germany, 1900–1920.

Austria and the Wiener Werkstätte

In Austria, the search for a new style at the beginning of the century was led by Josef Hoffman and key members of the Succession group, founded in 1897. The main objective of this group of Viennese artists and designers was to improve the status of the decorative arts. Members of the group were employed as teachers in the Vienna Museum of Applied Arts from 1899. A breakaway faction, including the painters Gustav Klimt, Olbrich, Moser and Hoffman, established the Wiener Werkstätte in 1903–4. This was a small colony of artists who wished to promote the individual creativity of the designer, in keeping with the beliefs of Van der Velde. They sought to move away from the dogma of mass-production extolled by German theorists and American industrialists. Their principles were closely allied to the British Arts and Crafts, and their designs had their stylistic roots in German Jugendstijl and French Art Nouveau.

—·◆·—

ABOVE
—
Georg Jensen is better remembered for his clean lines and abstract forms. His company led the field in contemporary silverware and jewelry in the first half of this century. Brooch, Denmark, c 1910.

Folk art in Scandinavia

During these years other European countries either reproduced the fashionable designs stemming from France, or they returned to their own indigenous folk arts for inspiration, looking for a naturalistic style to soften the edge of the new modernity. The Nordic countries of Sweden, Denmark, Finland and Norway drew on the idealized democratic principles of craft production, searching for an aesthetic formula that was in keeping with their cultural traditions. Nevertheless, they recognized the need to invite industrial sponsorship, not only to maintain links with the market place, but also to provide financial support for the designers. They hoped this would lead eventually to a greater dissemination of well-made goods. Some of the best examples of Scandinavian jewelry design of this period include the work of the Danish silversmith, Georg Jensen.

—·◆·—

BELOW AND FAR LEFT
—
Scandinavian design during this period was relatively formal. Silver clips, Georg Jensen, Denmark, 1930s.

René Lalique

(FRANCE, 1860–1945)

René Lalique, a Parisian goldsmith and jeweler, was trained by the goldsmith Louis Aucoc and travelled to England in the 1880s to study silversmithing. He was to have an important influence on European Art Nouveau design in the first decade of the twentieth century He exploited themes that characterized the flamboyance of La Belle Epoque, not only in his use of exotic materials, but also through the use of insect forms such as the dragonfly and lizard. These creations were inspired by the organic features of plant life, situated in a utopian, fantasy world that crossed the barrier between nineteenth-century historicism and the new forms developing from twentieth-century technology.

Like other designers working during this period, Lalique was mainly concerned with the reconciliation between the ideals of beauty and utility. His jewelry is charged with movement and emotional tension achieved with the imaginative juxtaposing of the differing qualities of glass, plique-à-jour enamelling, chrysophrase and gold materials.

Sinuous curves combine in a unified and rythmic whole. This results in an exciting inter-play between wearer and form. Sarah Bernhardt is perhaps one of the best known patrons of Lalique's work. It is significant that his jewelry, as a part of the decorative arts, stresses the individuality of the artist-craftsman at a time when many designers were coming to terms with exploiting and conforming to the joint pressures of manufacturing practice and collective thought.

Lalique's technical virtuosity and versatility is offset by the impact of colour and pagan symbolism. Plant and insect forms were combined as a part of the decoration and function. Several different objects were drawn together by the forcefulness of his style. Lalique utilized a delicate and luxurious vocabulary which typifies the artistic and inventive nature of French Art Nouveau.

A pendant brooch in diamond and tourmaline, offset by rich, plique-à-jour enamelling. René Lalique, France, late 1890s.

Liberty & Co.

(BRITAIN, C1875–)

Silver and enamel belt buckle designed by Jessie M King for Liberty & Co in 1906.

In 1875, Arthur Lasenby Liberty set up a shop in London, initially specializing in the importing and retailing of Oriental goods from India and Japan. Designers from the Arts and Crafts movement were employed to create innumerable products, from furniture and textiles to ceramics and silverware. The latter category was sold under the labels of 'Cymric' and 'Tudric' wares from the 1890s. These included a large collection of jewelry pieces designed and manufactured by individuals such as Jessie King, Archibald Knox, Rex Silver, Georgina and Arthur Gaskin, and Oliver Baker.

They were initially made by hand, although by the end of the nineteenth century silverware and jewelry were increasingly manufactured by machine and contracted out to various firms such as Haselers of Birmingham. They included brooches, pendants, belt clasps and necklaces. Few of these designs were intended for ceremonial or other formal occasions, contrasting with the importance attached to silver plate in the silversmithing, jewelry and allied trades.

These designers favoured the use of semi-precious stones such as peridot, olivine, tourmaline, moonstone and chrysoprase. In a few examples, precious stones such as rubies, sapphires, emeralds, fine pearls and diamonds were used. This was partly because of cost, but also because individual creativity took precedence over conforming to traditional aesthetic practices. Other materials were also popular and often utilized in varying combinations, such as glass and ceramic.

The market for such jewels was often limited to a more 'enlightened' and artistic clientele who appreciated the unusual aesthetic and moralistic qualities associated with dress reform in the late nineteenth century. Dress reform was concerned with the restricting nature of Victorian costume. In Britain, the Rational Dress Society was established in the 1870s. It campaigned against the wearing of corsets and preferred the adoption of simpler and looser garments that could be adorned with a large and eye-catching piece of jewelry, for example a robe clasp. There were important parallel developments in the United States with the foundation of the American Free Dress League.

The Tiffany Studios, New York:
The American Arts and Crafts Movement

(AMERICA, ESTABLISHED LATE 1830S)

Tiffany & Co, produced a prolific amount of jewelry from the latter half of the nineteenth century, first inspired both by British Arts and Crafts and later by Continental Art Nouveau in the first decade of the twentieth century. Louis Comfort Tiffany had been trained as an artist and in collaboration with Julia Munson he managed the jewelry department from 1903. He manufactured luxurious Byzantine-inspired wares, utilizing materials such as opals and amethysts reminiscent of the jewelry at Liberty & Co. in England.

The Tiffany Studios closed in 1916, although the company continues to produce fine jewelry today. When the studio halted production, there were a number of large companies such as Marcus & Co. who continued to emulate the Tiffany 'style'.

During this period, *The Craftsman* magazine extolled the virtues of simplicity and practicality. These beliefs were to influence the work of another artist-jeweler, Madeline Yale Wynne, who explored the artistic nature of different non-precious materials such as copper, pebbles and rock crystals, rather than the more usual preoccupations with precious and semi-precious metals and stones. This proved to be a much more enduring influence on future design than the Tiffany Studios, because of the search for new forms that indirectly reflected the modern world.

Other American craftsmen who practised within the Arts and Crafts arena included the silversmiths, Clemens Friedell, Janet Payne Bowles and Mildred Watkins, and the jewelers, Brainerd Bliss Thresher, Josephine Hartwell and Florence D. Koehler.

A swordfish brooch manufactured by Tiffanys during the 1930s in diamond, sapphires, emeralds and rubies.

Charles Ashbee and the Guild of Handicraft

(BRITAIN, 1863–1942)

The Guild of Handicraft was established in 1888 by Charles Ashbee in order to develop techniques and aesthetics in jewelry, as well as in furniture and metalwork. Ashbee was one of the first designers in the Arts and Crafts movement to experiment with jewelry. He produced a range of items at the Guild of Handicraft, including brooches and belt buckles. Initially, there were a few trained jewelers, other than those craftsmen that had worked in metals such as copper and silver. After 1900, however, skilled jewelry craftsmen became more involved within the Guild.

Their work was inspired by the fine craftsmanship and ideologies of the medieval period. It was essentially a reaction to the shoddy machine-made goods that had been created by industrialization in the late eighteenth and nineteenth centuries.

Charles Ashbee was trained as an architect, as well as a silversmith and jeweler. He provided a great many designs, typified by the famous peacock seen in much of his work, and was influenced by Cellini, perhaps the greatest goldsmith of the Italian Renaissance. Among other designers who produced jewelry at the Guild were Fred Partridge, whose work had much in common with French Art Nouveau in his use of horn and steel, and May Hart, the skilled enamelist, whom Partridge married.

C R Ashbee's pendant (gold, pearls, amethysts and moonstones) is a delicate, almost subdued design. England, 1902.

TWO

Art Deco

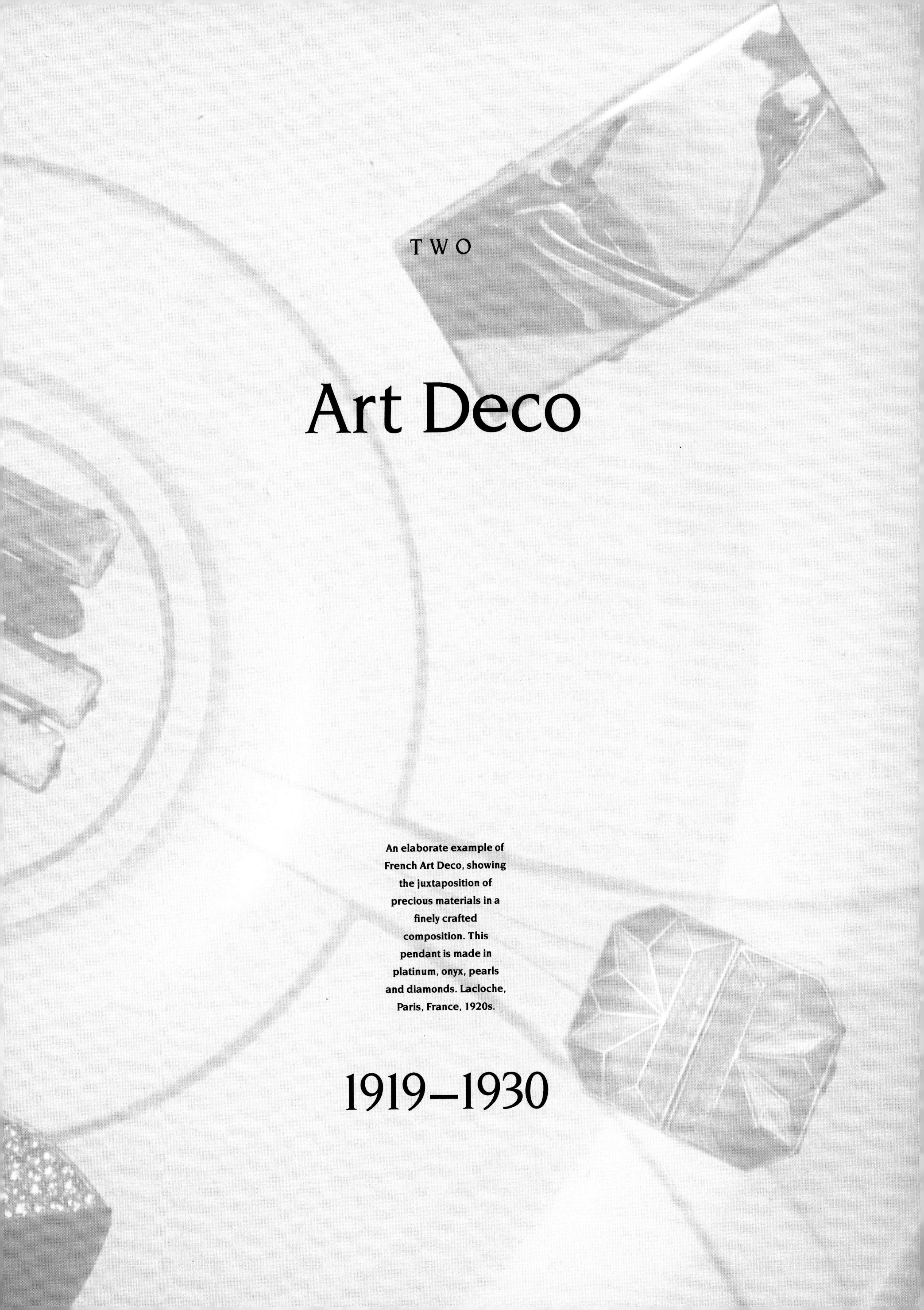

An elaborate example of
French Art Deco, showing
the juxtaposition of
precious materials in a
finely crafted
composition. This
pendant is made in
platinum, onyx, pearls
and diamonds. Lacloche,
Paris, France, 1920s.

1919–1930

BY THE TIME OF THE FIRST WORLD
War (1914–18) the last vestiges of the
nineteenth century had been swept away.
Where nineteenth century taste had revelled in excess, the economic and social
pressures which immediately followed the
war brought with them a new mood for a
rigorous and clean-cut modern look. This
period of stringency was, however, shortly
succeeded, in the 1920s, by a consumer
boom which affected all levels of society. It
saw industry flourishing, and brought with
it a mood of exuberant flamboyance. Art
Deco, as the characteristic style of this
period, contains within it an intriguing
contradiction that reflects these two contrasting postwar moods. On the one hand,
it is streamlined and ascetic, on the other it
has elements that can be seen as flashy or
frivolous. It is one of the most eclectic of all
styles, which is appropriate to the period
of rapid change and stark contrasts to which
it belongs.

—·◆·—

Art Deco style

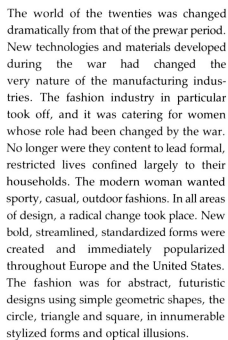

The world of the twenties was changed dramatically from that of the prewar period. New technologies and materials developed during the war had changed the very nature of the manufacturing industries. The fashion industry in particular took off, and it was catering for women whose role had been changed by the war. No longer were they content to lead formal, restricted lives confined largely to their households. The modern woman wanted sporty, casual, outdoor fashions. In all areas of design, a radical change took place. New bold, streamlined, standardized forms were created and immediately popularized throughout Europe and the United States. The fashion was for abstract, futuristic designs using simple geometric shapes, the circle, triangle and square, in innumerable stylized forms and optical illusions.

The term Art Deco was derived from the Paris *Exposition des Arts Decoratifs* in 1925, when the new style was at its height. A myriad of stylistic influences contributed to Art Deco. These included images of speed such as the greyhound and the gazelle, and of machinery, such as the automobile and the aeroplane. In addition there was the influence of the interest in Egyptology awakened by the discovery of Tutenkhamun's tomb in 1922. This led to the scarab beetle becoming a widely used symbol (jewelers incorporated it with tiger's eyes, turquoise and coloured crystals). The 'Cleopatra look' became *de rigeur* and was promoted by Hollywood actresses such as Anna Held, Claudette Colbert and Helen Gardner.

In America the Art Deco aesthetic was combined with other indigenous styles such as pre-Columbian, Mayan, Aztec and American Indian art. It became transformed into something more luxurious and decorative than its European counterpart, and was known as the zigzag style, epitomized by the tapered Chrysler Building in New York (1928–30).

ABOVE LEFT
—
Commercial tin designs, c 1925–1930, decorated in contemporary Art Deco fashion – a profile of a fashionable female figure, a common motif, that appeared in many designs, such as cigarette cases and compacts.

BELOW LEFT
—
This radiator grille from the Chanin building, New York, 1929, epitomizes the 'moderne' style of Art Deco, with a zig-zag and streamline effect.

—·◆·—

ABOVE
—
Pendant in frosted rock crystal, jade, lapis lazuli, diamonds, emeralds and mounted on platinum. Georges Fouquet, France, 1923–24.

RIGHT
—
Art Deco coral, onyx, jade and diamond tassel necklace by Georges Fouquet. France, 1925.

Art Deco jewelry

The First World War had a major effect on the jewelry trade. The precision equipment employed in jewelry making could be adapted with relative ease to gun part manufacture, and the market for new decorative jewelry which had flourished between 1900 and 1914 virtually dried up during the war. There was no importing or exporting of jewelry except on the black market.

During the 'Art Deco' period that followed the war, jewelry design was closely related to fine art, particularly in France, which was the cultural centre of Europe. Many artists and sculptors, including Picasso, Braque and Salvador Dali experimented with jewelry design, bringing the influence of Cubism and Futurism. Bevis Hillier relates Art Deco to Cubism in *The Style of the Century* in this way:

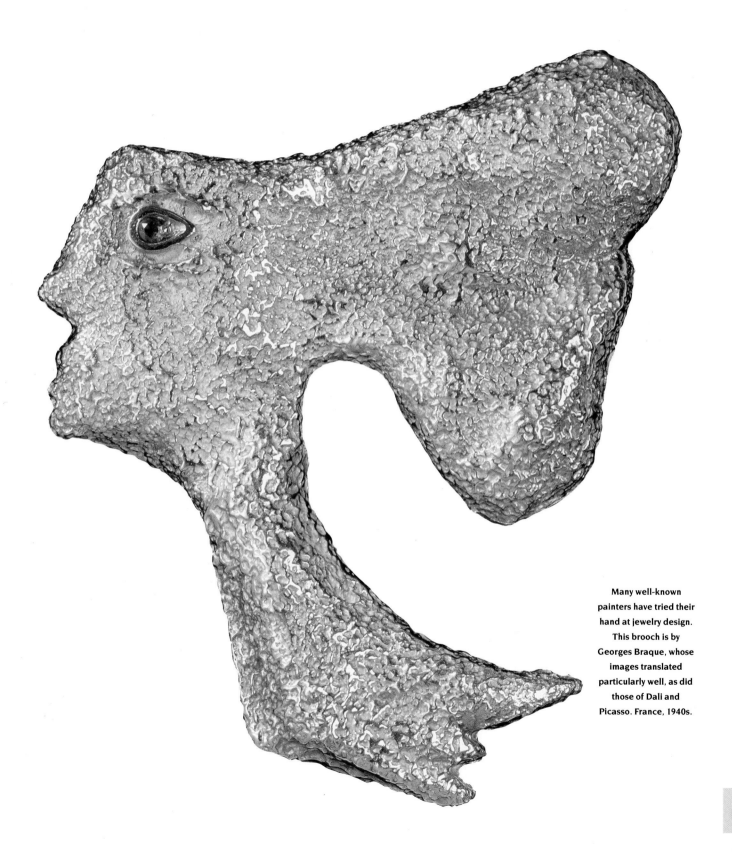

Many well-known
painters have tried their
hand at jewelry design.
This brooch is by
Georges Braque, whose
images translated
particularly well, as did
those of Dali and
Picasso. France, 1940s.

A thirties diamond bracelet, watch and clips set with coral and black onyx diamonds by an unknown maker.

'(Cubism) was a style which had nothing to do with anachronisms, pastiches or worn-out traditions. It was partly an attempt to reconcile art with a world that was speeding up and being fragmented . . . and translated into the prevailing mood of the 1920s (it) produced new conformations, fronds, bubbles, fissures, jagged outcroppings. The style now known as Art Deco was in essence tamed Cubism.'

Another thing to affect the world of jewelry design in this period was that the market had changed significantly. As well as the royal and aristocratic clients of the 19th century, there was now a market among the 'new rich' – families whose wealth had come from the Industrial Revolution. Inevitably this new variety of customer for expensive jewelry had a greater taste for modernity and innovation than had the old aristocratic market with its roots in a traditional past.

In response to the fashions and available technologies of the time, jewelers took up the Art Deco style, and started to use geometric shapes and polished surfaces. Precious stones were used less than before, and mainly for decorative effect.

TOP LEFT

Boucheron drop earrings in jade, onyx and diamonds. Boucheron was founded in 1858 and now has an extremely influential empire that spans the whole of western Europe and spreads as far east as Japan. Paris, France, 1920s.

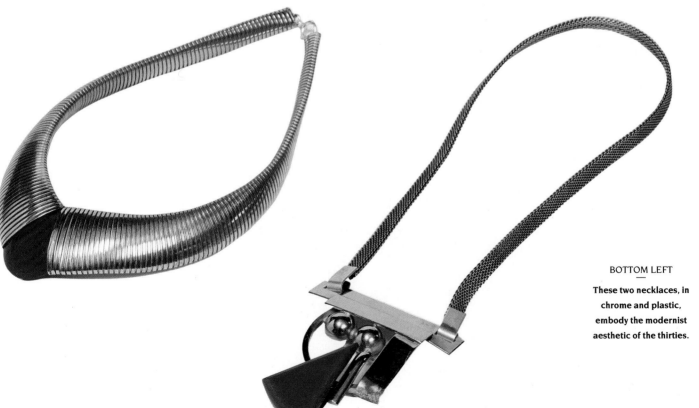

BOTTOM LEFT

These two necklaces, in chrome and plastic, embody the modernist aesthetic of the thirties.

The most sophisticated and chic Art Deco jewelry of the period was made in France, using combinations of materials such as coral and jade, and Japanese-inspired black enamel and marcasite. The most outstanding of the French artist-jewelers included Georges Fouquet, Raymond Templier, Gerard Sandoz, Jean Desprès and Jean Dunand. There were also a number of excellent copyists who took up the modern fashion.

Another French offshoot of the Art Deco style was a vogue for the "barbaric", inspired by the work of ancient goldsmiths. Designs in the barbaric style featured Islamic and Near Eastern patterns and mosaics. The Paris dancer, Josephine Baker, and society woman, Nancy Cunard, were the principal promoters of this style, wearing wide, plastic and lacquered bangles by Jean Dunand.

Compared with the French, English taste of the period was conservative. Jane Mulvagh in *Costume Jewelry in Vogue* said, 'Englishwomen of the twenties . . . who could afford such ornaments preferred something small but good – a string of pearls and possibly a regimental brooch in diamonds.' This taste for restraint was reflected in the comparatively delicate Art Deco designs of British jewelers working at the time. Even by this late stage, the Arts and Crafts influence was still apparent in the detailed, often floral settings of designers such as Sybil Dunlop and Carrie Francis. They specialized in decorative

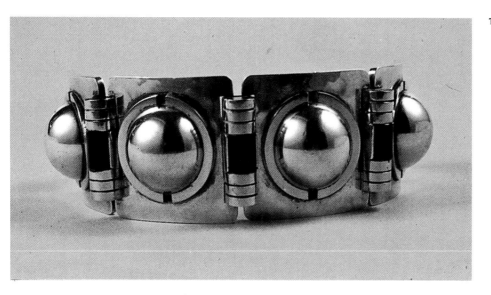

LEFT

This silver, silver-gilt and onyx bracelet is representative of the stark simplicity that characterized this period's obsession with the machine age. Jean Despres, Paris, 1930.

ABOVE

Cartier produced a number of 'wearable' time pieces which were worn by a fashionable clientele during the twenties and thirties. He is credited with the invention of the wrist watch in 1904 and this design from the late twenties is typical of the Art Deco period.

chains in silver, incorporating semi-precious stones such as moonstone, amethysts and topaz. Sybil Dunlop had been making jewelry since 1900. Much of her work was inspired by Celtic and Renaissance enamel-work. She favoured the use of moonstones and fire opals set within a wirework frame.

In America, the only near equivalent to the Art Deco artist-jewelers working in France and Britain were the anonymous designers who made pieces for the top of the Tiffany range. Otherwise in America the growth of Art Deco jewelry was inextricably linked to the boom in mass-produced costume pieces.

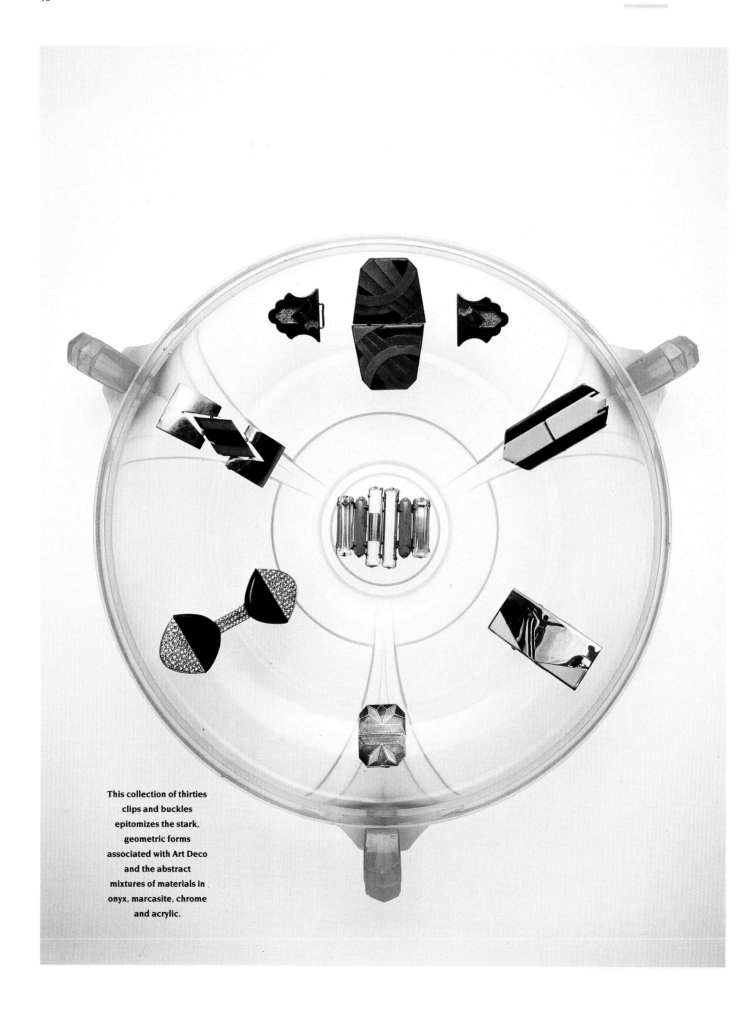

This collection of thirties clips and buckles epitomizes the stark, geometric forms associated with Art Deco and the abstract mixtures of materials in onyx, marcasite, chrome and acrylic.

Art Deco

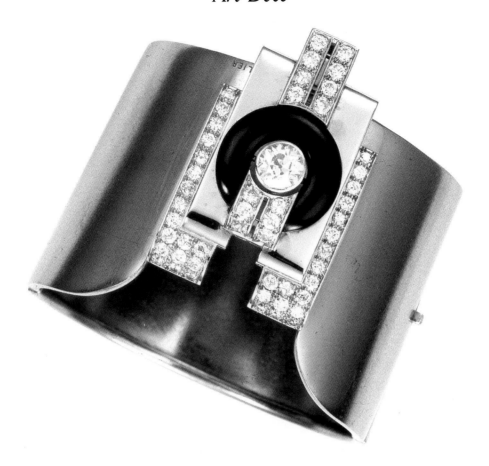

The first modern style to have a significant impact on European and American design was Art Deco, which had its origins in the French decorative arts of the 1920s.

Art Deco was to become a 'popular hallmark' in all aspects of design, particularly during the 1930s. Art Deco originates from the last traces of Art Nouveau, although it is much simpler in its effect and emphasizes the harmony of the interior.

There were numerous factors that influenced the impact of Art Deco, including the bright colours of the Ballet Russes, the formalist qualities of abstraction discovered by the Cubists and the impact of the decorative arts in general.

Numerous exhibitions contributed towards the general dissemination of the Art Deco style, especially the Paris International Exhibition of 1925. By the end of the decade, Art Deco had developed from a mixture of different elements. It was an 'assertively modern style', characterized by bold geometric and stylized patterns and representations of luxury, although it aimed to adapt designs to the requirements of mass production.

In England, Art Deco is characterized by the use of motifs like the sunburst, greyhound and pyramid-stepped forms that adorned every new building, domestic interior and the jewelry that was worn. In America, this decorative 'zigzag' style was associated with the riches and glamour of Hollywood and highlighted the need at that time to escape from the banality and poverty of the Depression during the thirties.

An Art Deco silver, platinum, gold, onyx and pave-set diamond panels bangle. Raymond Templier, France, c 1925–1930.

THREE

The Twenties and Thirties

Cartier ladybird brooch.
The House of Cartier was
founded in Paris about
1847 by Louis François
Cartier and became
established as the
world's finest 'court
jewelers'. After seeing
the Ballet Russes'
production of *Scheherezade*
in 1910, Cartier began
using semi-precious
stones, as well as the
usual fine gems.

1919–1930

THE END OF THE FIRST WORLD War marked the start of the popularity of costume jewelry. Fine jewelry at the time had unpleasant associations with being frivolous and unpatriotic. Jody Shields in *All That Glitters* quotes this contemporary comment: 'As the memory of the Great War and the profiteers sinks into oblivion, everyone wants to look as if "they belong" and it is by concealing the magnificence of their jewelry that they succeed, *Vogue* magazine featured tin and even shrapnel jewelry made by wounded soldiers, as well as patriotic accessories such as aviators' wings, regimental badges and victory flags.

The new fashions for women were casual and sporty, and were not well suited to the formality of precious gem stones. The Art Nouveau movement had already prompted a change in perception towards jewelry, focusing attention on aesthetic rather than monetary value, and in the postwar period it was the major couturiers who took this one stage further by initiating the trend for entirely non-precious jewelry.

— ·◆·—

Poiret, Chanel and the fashion accessory

The interest of the couturiers in costume jewelry had been initiated by Paul Poiret before the war, when he produced theatrical jewelry for Diaghilev's Ballet Russe in 1910. The bold, vivid Eastern silhouettes associated with this influential ballet were in stark contrast to the Art Nouveau styles of the time. Poiret later developed his range of costume jewelry further. He commissioned the fine jewelers René Boivin and Gripoix, and the artist, Paul Iribe, to accessorize his collections for European department stores as early as 1913. They produced the silk tassel-style jewelry, studded with semi-precious stones that typify Poiret's style. Other couturiers such as Chanel, Schiaparelli, Premet and Drescoll followed Poiret's lead.

Fashion magazines such as *Harper's Bazaar* and *Vogue* were at first cautious about the idea, as they relied heavily on advertising

revenue from fine jewelry houses such as Cartier. However, they overcame this trepidation and began to feature the new costume jewelry in the mid-1920s. Since there were no copyright laws at this time to prevent the Paris fashions being copied, other magazines throughout Europe and particularly America took up the theme and costume jewelry spread rapidly internationally.

The couturiers revelled in intricate detail and elaboration, particularly embroidered beadwork and garnitures which reflected current fashions, and the use of sequins and crystals that adorned evening wear. One of the most flamboyant and innovative of fashion designers was Coco Chanel, who coined the term 'junk' jewelry. She was

Cartier bracelet set with emerald of 76 carats, engraved with a verse from the Koran. Made to order by the Aga Khan III, 1930.

This brooch in gold, diamonds, onyx and enamel is typical of the strict geometric form and primary colour schemes of the Art Deco period.

the true advocate of fine 'fakery' and the 'deluxe poor look'. She believed that 'when you wear jewels, they should be visible, striking . . . (and you should) wear your real ones at home or amongst friends, not on the street. You should not wear your fortune around your neck as if you were a savage.' Chanel worked in collaboration with many people including Count Etienne de Beaumount and the Sicilian painter Fulco Santostefatto della Cerda in producing costume jewelry in the 1920s.

By 1925, the fashion was well-established, and the imitation of costly materials was no longer seen as a disgrace. In 1927 *Vogue* reported that 'Fashion has decided that all we need ask of an ornament is to adorn us, and that neither our complexions [suntans were newly fashionable] nor our gems are to be natural'.

In Germany, Pforzheim remained a major centre of jewelry production. At the beginning of the twentieth century German manufacturers had begun making fashion and hair accessories. The companies of Florein Grossé and Heinrich Henkel branched out into costume jewelry in the early twenties.

Likewise in the States, Coro (Cohn Rosenberger), later Corocraft, Richilieu, Miriam Haskell, Napier Incorporated (the oldest fashion jewelry house), Gustav Trifari and Carl Fishel began producing costume accessories such as handbag clasps, shoe buckles and hair ornaments. Fishel and Trifari were among the first jewelers to realize that the short bob (popularized in France) would spell death to their enormous range of hair ornaments. In response to this, they set up as costume jewelers under the name Trifari, Kraussman and Fishel.

Twenties fashions dictated a new range of ornaments. As well as the bob haircut, there were the dropped waistlines, rising and falling hemlines, and décolleté necklines or backless dresses, requiring a new range of jewelry styles. Costume jewelry expanded accordingly to include clips, liberty pins (to hold up corsetless lingerie), and free-flowing sautoirs associated with the dropped waistline.

—·◆·—

America and mass-produced jewelry

Very quickly novelty and trinket manufacturers began to produce copies of couturier costume pieces, which developed the market for fashion jewelry. America, in particular, was well placed to apply the new manufacturing techniques to the jewelry field, and where Paris had led the trend for costume jewelry, it was America that chiefly propagated it. Less hide-bound by craft traditions than the European countries, and less inhibited by old bureaucracies and stylistic inertia, America was undergoing full-scale industrialization. In the jewelry field America ceased simply to import or copy European role models and began to experiment with new technologies and materials of its own, to the extent that jewelry manufacture rapidly became a major industry. The *New York Times* pointed out in 1929 (ironically, since this was the year of the Wall Street Crash): 'Our jewelry industry has attained a position of economic dignity and importance.' Companies along the length of the East Coast, from New York City to Providence, Rhode Island, such as Napier and Co., were involved in jewelry production. They made silver giftware and also supplied jewelry props to Hollywood movie productions such as the *Ziegfeld Follies* show, *Samson and Delilah*, and *The Ten Commandments*. Lightness and simplicity were the qualities aspired to, and new materials came into their own, particularly plastics.

—·◆·—

H G Murphy's stunning silver necklace and pendant, set with a teardrop crystal, moonstones, pink coral and pearls. Britain, 1920s.

Plastic jewelry

The widespread introduction of synthetic plastics during the 1920s marked the beginning of jewelry that was affordable to the masses. Even though plastic in the early twenties was not yet a particularly cheap material, plastic jewelry did not have the couturier name attached to it which enhanced the prices of other costume jewelry. In addition, manufacturers at this stage began importing cheaper materials to combine with the plastic pieces, such as stones and crystal beads from Czechoslovakia, France and Germany, excellent fake pearls from Japan and glass mosaic from Italy.

Plastic was a material ideally suited to machine production and to the new clean-cut, geometric Art Deco styles. As Pulos says in *The American Design Ethic*, 'The action of instruments and machines was essentially geometric, as were the forms of the materials'. Plastic could be easily moulded into sharply defined shapes and it offered the possibility of 'mathematical precision and purity of finish'.

One well-known exponent of Art Deco plastic jewelry was an American, George F. Berklander from Providence, Rhode Island. He produced bar pins studded in rhinestone (which was very popular during this period). It is likely that he developed the first cellulose acetate flower pins as well as 'celluloid elephant chains for the wives of Presidents Harding and Coolidge: and tiny celluloid airplanes with Lindbergh's name on them'.

To start with, there was debate as to whether jewelry, with its ancient craft traditions, ought to take on such entirely different contemporary materials and production methods, but inevitably it did adapt to this new chapter in its history.

The development of synthetic plastics had begun in the late nineteenth century when they were seen as substitutes for more expensive natural materials such as horn, ivory and tortoiseshell. Several different types were produced such as Cellulose (1867), Casein (1897) and Bakelite (1907). However it was not until the 1920s that plastics were developed which were sufficiently practical to mould and colour to

A collection of jewelry in plastic and chrome from the twenties and thirties.

This pendant in silver gilt
and semi-precious
stones is a fine piece of
arts and crafts inspired
design. Sybil Dunlop,
England, 1920s.

be of real use in jewelry making. As soon as such plastics did become available manufacturers started to produce large quantities of beads, bangle bracelets and moulded pins with a variety of different finishes from mottled to pearlized effects. Pearl imitations were mass-produced from the mid-1920s.

Bakelite had been used commercially from 1910, primarily as an insulator for electrical goods. It was Reicholds in the USA who first used it, under the name of Catalin, for the manufacture of costume jewelry. It was light, warm, virtually indestructible and extremely well suited to the imitation of a number of different substances, particularly pearls. From the late 1920s onwards it could be produced in more sophisticated colours, was given a better lustre, and could be marbled in ways that did not fade in sunlight. Its refractive properties were excelled only by the diamond and it made an excellent substitute for jade, cornelian and goldstone. It was not just an inferior imitation of natural materials, but had many qualities unique to itself.

On the whole, novelty plastic jewelry was purchased by those who were looking for cheerful, but inexpensive items. It did not achieve the relative cachet that Chanel had brought to certain other types of costume jewelry.

— · ◆ · —

The thirties

In the 1930s, the glamour and extravagance of the twenties gave way, particularly in America, to increasing economic hardship and to the Depression. This had a number of different effects on the jewelry trade. On the one hand, people were less able to afford expensive jewelry, and so the costume jewelry market was comparatively thriving, while many of the fine jewelry houses suffered serious financial losses. One contemporary journal, *Art Plastic*, commented that all the main department stores in New York, including Saks and Bonwits were selling 40 to 50 per cent costume jewelry during this period. On the other hand, those who could afford more expensive pieces adopted a conservative attitude, rejecting the novelty and experimental designs of the previous decade in favour of safer, more traditional jewelry. These designs represented reassurance in a financially threatened society, and could be seen as a relatively secure form of investment. By complete contrast, a third type of jewelry to emerge against the political and economic background of the 1930s was an extreme and bizarre style inspired by the Dadaist and Surrealist art movements.

— · ◆ · —

Costume jewelry

At this time manufacturers were producing three distinct types of costume jewelry. There were couture originals, their copies, and mass-produced trinkets, which sold through outlets such as the five and dime stores in the United States and their Woolworths counterparts in Britain. The originals were usually made on the Continent and copied in America more cheaply, because of the high taxes imposed on foreign-made products. The copies usually included rhinestones, semi-precious gems that were set by hand and artificial pearls made of Bakelite. It was an important status symbol to wear the couturier original before it was copied and became widely available.

Diamond and black onyx bow brooch. France, 1920s–30s.

Many of the fine jewelry houses were forced by the economic depression to turn to producing costume jewelry. This resulted in a much closer relationship between the two sides of the trade. Standards of workmanship for costume jewelry consequently improved greatly, as did its reputation. A higher degree of artistic daring also became apparent in the costume jewelry field. The traditional glamour of white gold combined with diamonds was transformed into costume jewelry by Trifari, who produced cane tops, glove and dress clips and gilt chain bracelets. Fine jewelry houses like Cartier and Herz followed suit.

The thirties marked the heyday of Hollywood, and costume jewelry was promoted and popularized by many of the leading film stars, in particular Mae West.

Plastic jewelry became fully integrated into the fashion arena during the thirties, by when the fashion magazines had really begun to recognize the importance of this market. The manufacture of plastic jewelry was still very labour intensive. Hand-finishing operations did not cease until the 1940s, which kept the price of cast plastics relatively high.

From 1931, acrylics were being produced as a coating agent and safety bonding for glass in Germany, and within a short time they were adopted for use in jewelry. Acrylic is easy to colour, and renowned for its clarity, making it an ideal material for non-precious jewelry. It could be carved, faceted and engraved just like a crystal. It is known under two trade names today, Lucite and Plexiglas. The patent for Lucite was bought up by a costume jewelry manufacturer in New York, called Meyer Bros, in 1941.

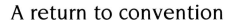

A return to convention

The thirties were a period highlighted by a return to a conservative attitude towards jewelry and the status symbolism associated with it. There was a renewed interest in the idea of 'good taste' and morally acceptable styles. One important modification made at this time was the introduction of interchangeable stones in order to match different costumes without the expense and extravagance of commissioning new designs.

The thirties are characterized by a soft but streamlined look. Curved, feminine fashions superceded the hard-edged lines of Art Deco. In terms of jewelry fashion, clips were particularly popular and were often combined to make a brooch. They were considered an essential part of women's dress. The fashion for diamonds was at its height, whether real or paste, and flower sprays and bouquet jewelry with gilded finishes were a favourite design.

Cartier clock, bracelet and ladybird brooch. France, 1920s–30s.

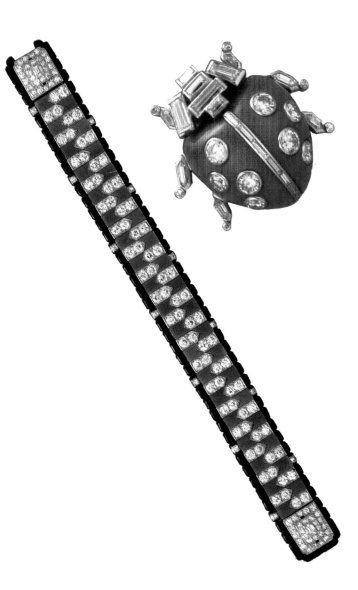

**Brooch and bracelet, in
ruby and diamonds, by
Van Cleef and Arpels.
France, 1930s.**

Dadaism and Surrealism

In sharp contrast with this return to safe forms of design were the avant-garde contemporary art movements, known as Dadaism and Surrealism. These movements had a considerable impact on the world of jewelry. Their ideas were embraced by designers such as Chanel's fashion rival, Schiaparelli. In addition a number of the Dadaist and Surrealist artists themselves experimented with jewelry design, including Salvador Dali, Max Ernst, Jean Clement and Jean Arp.

Dali designed a pair of telephone earrings as well as necklaces made from locks, clips and paperweights in Plexiglas. Clement's passion thermometers indicated a lover's temperament.

Surrealism considered the whole spectrum of human activity. It was concerned with the unconscious mind and the power of dreams. The Surrealist artists were inter-ested in how the imagination could be harnessed and expressed in the most 'primitive state'. Aesthetically, this resulted in the recording of dream images with strong Freudian (sexual) undertones and visual puns.

Schiaparelli came up with some of the most extraordinary Surrealist jewelry designs during the thirties and forties. These included a vinyl collar, embedded with multi-coloured metal insects, a pink ice cube necklace, buttons in the form of musical notes, hatchet- and heart-shaped brooches and diamond-studded false finger nails. These strong visual statements expressed the Surrealist movement's contempt for convention.

Surrealism reached its peak at the Paris Exhibition of 1936 with a range of bizarre items on display, from lantern-lit jewelry to glassless spectacles. They were admired by the social and fashionable elite of this period including Mae West and Mrs Reginald Fellows.

— . ◆ . —

Chanel and costume jewelry

French costume jewelry, probably Chanel, from the late 1940s/early 1950s.

The gradual introduction of costume jewelry in the early twentieth century is clearly associated with the more functionalist and modernist style. By the eve of the First World War, elaborate and delicate jewelry characteristic of the Edwardian period was replaced by much larger and simpler pieces.

Seasonal costume jewelry finally came into its own and this owed much to the work of two influential fashion designers of the period, Gabrielle Chanel and Elsa Schiaparelli. They removed the stigma of wearing fake jewels, from items of pure imitation to the celebration of 'stylishness . . . and nonchalant luxury'.

Chanel is important, not only because she 'invented' costume jewelry, but also because she used these unusual designs to complement her own fashion collections. She believed that the concept of 'fake' should be used as a symbol of confidence for the new independent woman of the twenties, since the wearing of precious jewelry was looked down as being frivolous and unpatriotic, particularly after the war.

New fashions in dress design also demanded a different kind of function in jewelry. Long lengths of pearl robe, glass beads or sautoirs accentuated long, lean lines and sleeveless evening dresses left arms uncovered to be decorated in numerous bangles.

Costume jewelry was not only influenced by biannual fashion changes, but also contemporary art movements, including the work of individuals such as Picasso, Arp and Braque, who also designed jewelry themselves. They developed a taste for ethnic fashions, epitomised by Nancy Cunard's huge 'slave' bangles in African ivory.

RIGHT

Fifties costume jewelry in paste, cuff, bangle and earrings by Coppola and Toppo for Schiaparelli.

FOUR

The Second World War and After

This curious choice of
subject matter indicates
just how pervasive the
artwork of the surrealists
became. Cactus brooch,
in enamel, rubies and
diamonds, by an
unknown maker. Paris,
France, 1940s.

1939–1949

A thirties silver and
marcasite brooch from
Germany.

IN THE SECOND WORLD WAR, AS IN the First, many European jewelers found themselves involved in the war effort. Their workshops and precision tools were used for the manufacture of bullets, surgical steel equipment and radio components. Another factor that suppressed jewelry making during the war was the shortage of gold and silver bullion and of other materials, as well as labour shortages. Costume jewelry remained unrationed but even that was not widely available. Many of the major European centres of production were bombed, including Birmingham and Pforzheim. With the exception of a few crudely made pieces, experimental plastic jewelry designs ceased during the war period. Manufacturers turned out large quantities of regimental badges, while there was a renewed interest in Victoriana, such as Whitby jet (mourning jewelry) and Berlin iron jewelry.

— · ◆ · —

The postwar period

In Britain and the rest of Europe, the consequences of the war were to last many years, as shortages of manpower and materials continued and the painstaking work of reconstruction took place, much of it financed by America. Many of the technological and scientific advances made during the war were adapted for peacetime purposes. Automated manufacturing processes, the development of new plastics and the emergence of microchip technology, among other innovations, were all to have profound effects. In 1946 the 'Britain Can Make It' exhibition sought to stimulate all branches of trade and commerce, by showing how war technology could be effectively employed for civilian product manufacture.

The war had brought with it a greater distribution of wealth and increased economic independence for women. Many women had worked during one or both of the wars and, although they were now encouraged to return to the roles of housewife and mother, there were those who wanted, as well as those who needed, to return to work. Fashions became more casual, and the choice of ready to wear clothes increased considerably.

New influences on design

After the war, there was a new appreciation in Europe of the importance of design as a means of selling products in the increasingly competitive commercial world. This was an idea that had been first preached by American industrial designers of the 1930s, who had begun to put as much thought into the styling of a product as into its practicality. In the industrial reconstruction that took place in Europe after the war, this message began to play an important part, particularly in view of the increasingly international markets in which manufacturers were having to compete. It was important to make one's product attractive in order for it to hold its own against foreign competitors. Rapid industrial growth brought with it a wave of new design practices and debate.

The curving, clean lines of this bracelet are distinctive of Danish design. It is softly organic in essence, but with a pure simplicity of form. A Tilander, Denmark, 1930/40.

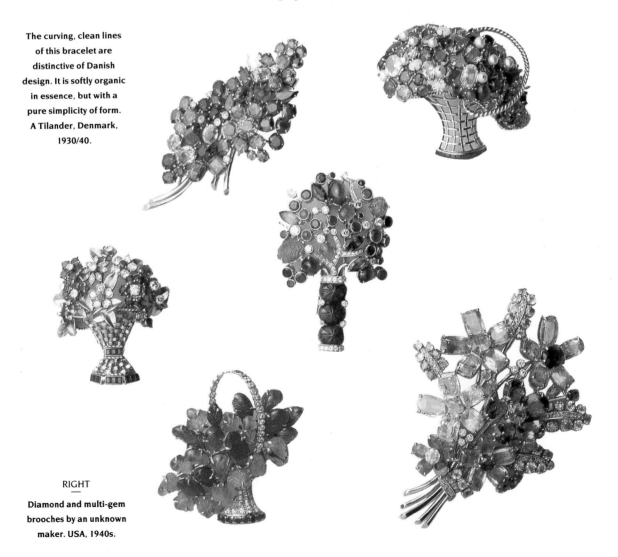

RIGHT
—
Diamond and multi-gem brooches by an unknown maker. USA, 1940s.

Another major design influence of the period was the Bauhaus. This was an educational institution set up in Weimar in Germany under the directorship of the architect Walter Gropius, in 1919. The Bauhaus developed ideas concerning the 'machine aesthetic'. The Nazis closed the school in 1933, but in 1937 it was reinstated at the Chicago School of Design, where Moholy-Nagy returned to the original teaching principles of the old school. After the war, the school continued to be a source of influence on designers, including jewelers.

Naturally, the discovery of new plastics was to have a major influence on designs of the postwar period. The most important ones to emerge were PVC (vinyl), mela-mine, polythene, polystyrene and nylon. Sylvia Katz has described the youth of this time as the 'first plastics generation, with their Terylene shirts, moulded (pleated) polyester skirts, beehive hairdos sealed in position with vinyl acetate lacquer and legs encased in "sheerer era" nylon stockings suspended from synthetic rubber Lycra roll-ons'. The development of metal alloys and numerous acrylic plastics and injection moulded plastics (a cheap replacement for glass beads) increased the variety of plastics on the market. Manufacturers began to look to the Far East, particularly Hong Kong and Korea, for cheap supplies of raw materials. New machinery made the mass production of components more efficient.

— ◆ —

The jewelry trade

In the past, the jewelry trade had usually lagged behind the fashion industry by as much as 10 or 15 years. However, this time lag had begun decreasing with the introduction of mass-produced jewelry in the twenties and thirties, and by the end of the Second World War the jewelry trade was able to respond quickly to changing fashions.

Established houses such as Boucheron, Van Cleef and Arpels, Lacloche and Cartier, continued to thrive in the immediate post-war years. The American jewelers and New York branches of Parisian houses such as Paul Flato, Vedura and Traebert and Hoeffer flourished too, because they had not been directly involved in the traumas of occupied Europe.

This was a period when costume jewelers felt free to experiment with base metals, silver gilt and paste, and when the artist-jeweler came back into prominence.

— ◆ —

LEFT AND BELOW RIGHT

These three brooches are characterized by asymmetry, indicated by natural sweeping, flora and fauna. Sterle of Paris, France, 1940s.

RIGHT

These clip brooches, gold set with diamonds, were designed by the well-known firm of Lacloche. Paris, France, 1940.

Jewelry design

During the drab years of austerity that followed the war, jewelry design continued
to develop, despite the economic difficulties. The streamlined and geometric lines
of Art Deco design gave way to softer, more
voluptuous shapes. Jewelry from the late
forties was extremely colourful, in sharp
contrast to the monotony of the 'utility'
designs produced during the war.

Forties jewelry is characterized by its
chunkiness and use of contrast. The fashion
was nicknamed 'cocktail style' and it con-
tained a mixture of elements, formal and
informal, natural and unnatural, 'stiff and
fluid (outlines), static yet full of movement'.
The interest in machinery which was widespread at the time, with the rapid growth
in industrial production, is reflected in the
jewelry designs.

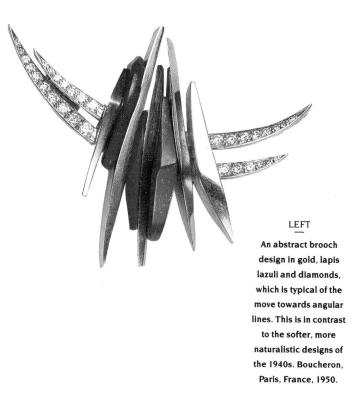

LEFT

An abstract brooch
design in gold, lapis
lazuli and diamonds,
which is typical of the
move towards angular
lines. This is in contrast
to the softer, more
naturalistic designs of
the 1940s. Boucheron,
Paris, France, 1950.

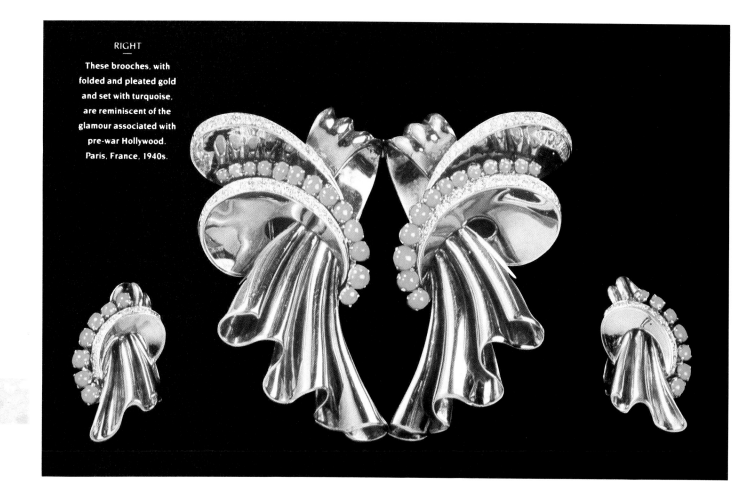

RIGHT

These brooches, with
folded and pleated gold
and set with turquoise,
are reminiscent of the
glamour associated with
pre-war Hollywood.
Paris, France, 1940s.

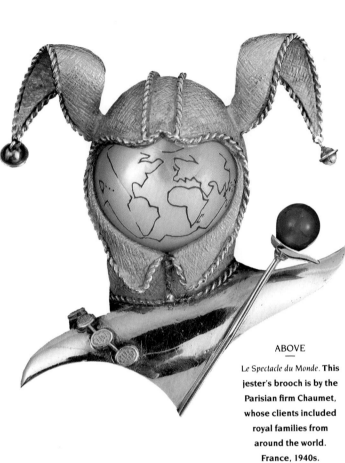

ABOVE

Le Spectacle du Monde. **This jester's brooch is by the Parisian firm Chaumet, whose clients included royal families from around the world. France, 1940s.**

ABOVE

A bag clip in steel and enamel by an unknown maker. France, 1940s.

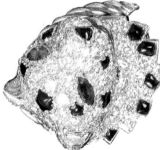

RIGHT

Leopards and panthers covered with pave-set gemstones became famous in the 1940s thanks to the collection produced by Cartier of Paris.

The chunkiness of forties work is indicative of the desire at this period to exude wealth despite the fact that most people did not have the financial resources to buy fine jewelry. In consequence limited quantities of gold would be carefully wrought in order to give the illusion of being larger than they really were.

Figurative forms were popular, set against large expanses of metals in exotic colours such as rose pink. This was a much more fluid style than Art Deco, with pleats and drapes simulating the folds of a piece of fabric.

There were also flower sprays made with invisible settings in which small-cut rubies and sapphires were placed. There were a number of experiments made during this period with unusual motifs such as clowns, ballerinas and wild cats. Cartier helped build up the taste for exotic fauna, in particular the wild cats designed by Jeanne Toussaint. These animals became the 'luxurious but poignant symbols of the Duchess of Windsor' and were perfected by Cartier during the forties and fifties.

— · ◆ · —

Fine art jewelry

Many fine artists continued to see jewelry making as an important element in their work. They continued the move to discover imaginative and creative forms, to which the intrinsic value of the materials used was subordinate. Unlike the specialist jewelry houses they did not always lay great store by technical perfection. An exception in this was the Italian artist, Gio Pomodoro, who took great care in working his materials. He combined decorativeness with function in a highly successful way. His brother, Arnaldo, worked with him. Another important Italian contribution to jewelry design was the work of Bruno Martinazzi. Martinazzi experimented with the layering effects of gold, with a strong emphasis on texture.

Other painters and sculptors who took an interest in jewelry included Braque, Tanguy, Man Ray, Dali, Dubuffet, Picasso, Fontana, Giacometti and Alexander Calder.

TOP LEFT
—
A *Goldfinger* **bracelet designed by the Italian Figurative-jeweler Bruno Martinazzi, 1969.**

BOTTOM LEFT
—
Diamond, ruby and cultured pearl bangle, and pearl and diamond bangle by Boucheron. Enamel and diamond bracelet designed by Jean Schlumberger for Tiffany. USA, 1940s.

RIGHT
—
A Jo Mazer bracelet, brooch and earrings in diamonds, gold and emeralds. USA, late 1940s.

A fifties arabesque bracelet and earrings in gold and gems by Har.

The Surrealists produced many amusing brooches in zoomorphic and anthropomorphic forms. Dali said of his work:

'My jewels are a protest against the high cost of jewelry materials. My aim is to show the jeweler's art in its true perspective – where the design and craftsmanship are of more value than the gems.'

Even Georges Braque continued to design jewelry during this period. He translated many of the principles of his paintings into three-dimensional precious forms which brought out 'the metaphysical and magical aspects' of the material.

One of the seminal artist-jewelers in America at this period was Margaret de Patta. She had attended the Bauhaus summer school in Chicago in 1940 and was influenced by its ideas. She specialized in finding new catches and earring fittings, and in the exciting use of new materials. She used stainless steel and plastic in her work and began producing prototypes for manufacture in 1946, because she could not keep pace with the demand for her work. It was in keeping with her social views to create cheaper pieces that would be widely affordable.

**This Georges Braque
ring is an international
abstract design in 18
carat gold. France, 1960.**

Costume jewelry

The decreasing supplies of natural materials and the introduction of new plastics and technologies all fostered the continuing growth of the costume jewelry market after the war. Aspreys produced a highly successful brooch in 'washable plastic', but on the whole the attitude towards new materials was more conservative in Britain than it was in France and America where costume jewelry was more wholeheartedly embraced. Parisians loved 'faux gems' and many French couturiers encouraged the use of bold, but essentially classic designs. Christian Dior, who created the 'New Look' in 1947, developed the theatrical qualities of costume jewelry.

Tiffanys produced a number of novelty brooches, such as this monkey design, during the post-war period, a humorous touch in the drab years of austerity following World War 2. New York, USA, 1960.

Alexander Calder

(AMERICA, 1899–1976)

The artist, Alexander Calder, was the inventor of the sculptural mobile back in the early thirties, initially powered by motors and later by air currents. He was successful with jewelry at a time when many artists produced a rather watered-down version of their fine art paintings.

He managed to handle beaten copper and silver without the aid of conventional tools of the trade, producing a prolific range of items from hair combs to bracelets and brooches, which he exhibited for the first time in 1940 at the Willard Gallery in New York. After the war, his work was marked by a more spindly style associated with the fifties, although visually forceful enough to echo the sharp, zigzag motifs of the forthcoming electronics age, the so-called 'electrocardiogram' of the fifties.

Margret de Patta

(AMERICA, 1903–1964)

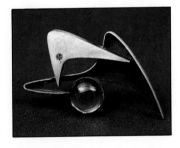

The design for this silver and quartz crystal brooch was developed from Margret de Patta's studies in painting and sculpture during the 1920s and reinforced by her work with the ex-Bauhaus photographer and artist Lazlo Moholy-Nagy. USA, 1947.

De Patta's jewelry is inspired by the aesthetics of the Bauhaus and particularly the teachings and work of the Hungarian artist, Lazlo Moholy-Nagy, whom she met at a summer school in 1940.

She began producing jewelry from 1929, having studied painting at the Academy of Fine Arts in San Diego (1921–23), the California School of Fine Arts (1923–25) and the Art Students League (1926–29).

She experimented with materials outside the traditional sphere of jewelry design at that time, by using stainless steel and plastic in her work, as well as the reflective qualities of stones with new cuts. From 1946, she began producing jewelry prototypes for mass production, which in turn proved to be a successful competitor to costume jewelry at that time.

Margaret de Patta contributed much towards jewelry by way of the Metal Arts Guild and the American Crafts Council, as well as becoming an important figure in the prehistory of contemporary American jewelry design.

FIVE

The Growth of Popular Culture

A ring, in 18 carat gold
and moonstones, by
Henning Koppel for
Jensen. Denmark, 1960.

1950–1965

A Miriam Haskell brooch,
USA, 1950s.

BY THE 1950s MOST OF THE BASIC postwar reconstruction in Western Europe (in the areas of housing, education and health) had taken place and a new 'consumer boom' began, with a demand for more choice and more high fashion styles. A combination of high employment, falling production costs and expanding markets contributed to this economic change. The boom affected all levels of society, particularly working class youth who were the target of major advertising campaigns.

Entertaining became very important during this decade, which helped the fashion trades to thrive. As Jody Shields has observed,

'The chic get-up of the 1950s was slightly sinister: false eyelashes, knife-sharp stiletto heels and stockings stencilled with leopard patterns . . . where the *femme fatale* and suburban woman came together was over the casserole. Entertaining, 1950s-style, was centred around the new technological wonder (this is more true in America) . . . In cities and suburban sub-divisions, (casual) soirees represented a revolutionary concept of hospitality, and fashion and jewelry styles evolved to accommodate this new informal way of life.'

The casual attitude to life she describes was most evident in Italy and America. Role models such as the movie stars Audrey Hepburn popularized it further.

America had an enormous influence on the new market throughout the fifties. It was from the United States that all types of cultural ideas and aspirations were disseminated, from rock 'n' roll to the huge new choice of consumer products – be it lawn mowers, dishwashers or, most influential of all, television. A wide array of 'space-age' items were produced to entice the customer, particularly the newly important teenage market. The contemporary style of the 1950s, which was applied to everything, was for sculptural and quirky shapes in bright pastel and primary colours. Thomas Hines in *Populuxe* describes this period as one of exuberant popular materialism: 'Things were not only more common and more available than before, they were invested with greater meaning . . . As in most periods, mass tastes during the postwar years were often at odds with what was considered good taste, or educated taste . . . it is an expression of outright, thoroughly vulgar joy in being able to live well.'

A Miriam Haskell collection of jewelry in gold and pearls, USA, 1950s.

Costume jewelry

This new fashion-conscious era expanded the market for costume jewelry. Decorative and amusing ornamentation became an essential. Even Chanel had crept out of retirement to reinvigorate the market with 'multi-layers of gilt, glass stones and pearls.' Chanel-inspired Renaissance jewelry remained in vogue well into the sixties. Christian Dior's jewelry designs during the fifties were increasingly produced by his protégé, Yves Saint Laurent.

There was a high level of competition amongst the retailing outlets of costume jewelry. The couture houses and leading manufacturers such as Napier, Corocraft and Trifari competed fiercely with one another, and started using the type of marketing techniques and outlets adopted by the cosmetics industry. Adrian Mann was one of the first costume jewelry wholesalers in Britain. He, and the other suppliers, started to popularize their goods with increased attention to excellent packaging and advertising.

The introduction of 'poppet' plastic beads in the early fifties offers an excellent example of how effectively new cheap jewelry fashions could spread throughout the Western market, using some of the outlets of the cosmetics trade. The beads were patented by Geoffrey Charles and sold through Walter Scaife Limited in the USA and Elizabeth Arden in Britain. In some respects they were the first truly 'popular' jewelry item.

Another favourite form of jewelry at the time was the 'bone-crunching' charm bracelet. This was known as the 'democratic accessory' and was worn by America's First Lady, Mamie Eisenhower. Charms were purchased to commemorate special occasions, or more personal motifs could be bought. Some were mass-produced to promote new hobbies and interests, including popular music and flower gardening.

Ankle bracelets were available for the first time as a variation on the wrist variety, and furry button earrings were produced as a cheaper, Surrealistic alternative to ones made from precious materials.

Cat, Coro, USA, 1940s;
tortoise, Corocraft,
USA, 1950s.

—·◆·—

A dragon brooch for the
costume jewelers Trifari,
USA, 1950s.

'Suburban' jewelry

A more conservative type of contemporary
jewelry design was that produced for the
mid-town suburban market that rose to
prominence in the mid-fifties. Some truly
unremarkable jewels were produced for the
middle-class housewife of suburban
America and this type of unadventurous
design spread from there to the equivalent
market in Europe.

— · ◆ · —

The artist-jewelers

In contrast with the traditional jewelry houses who were concentrating increasingly on gem-set extravagances, a new division of the jewelry trade began to make its mark in the 1950s. This was the rise of the artist-jeweler. At this period the artist-jewelers worked particularly in silver. Their designs echoed some of the newly discovered molecular structures that had been illustrated at the New York World Fair in 1939 and the Festival of Britain in 1951.

In America, the artist-jewelers were especially flourishing. Many of them were Europeans who had been teaching at the Bauhaus and had been forced to flee to America during the war. Bauhaus ideology became a major factor in postwar design debate, breaking down the boundaries between the fine and decorative arts. The work of several of the designers of the time is hard to fit into any traditional jewelry category. Sam Kramer's pieces,

TOP RIGHT
—
Sam Kramer produced a series of wild and crazy jewelry from the late 1930s, when he moved to Greenwich, New York. The brooch combines gold, silver, garnet, peridot and citrine and the design was inspired by science-fiction comics. USA, 1947.

BOTTOM RIGHT
—
A Trifari brooch. USA, 1940s.

RIGHT
—
A Trifari necklace in gold and pearls. USA, 1950s.

A Trifari necklace and
earrings. USA, mid–
1940s–1950s.

for example, incorporate found objects,
'aping other contemporary American fine
artists who were using the sculptural and
painterly technique of assemblage' (Vivien
Becker, *Jewellery*). From 1939 onwards
Kramer had a shop in Greenwich Village
in New York, where he explored the ideas
current in the world of fine art, particularly
abstract expressionism. During the fifties
and early sixties his work became increasingly abstract. He put a great emphasis on
texture, creating rocky formations and
rough-edged contours that were in complete contrast with the smooth-faceted cuts
used by the traditional jewelry trade.

The Swedish vernacular

Design in Scandinavia followed its own individualist path, founded on their continuing craft tradition, their democratic principles and their enduring respect for the materials they used. An exhibition held in Halsinborg in 1955 exemplified how the Swedish home was to be a microcosm of economical and socially egalitarian ideals. Their design styles became increasingly influential throughout the rest of Europe, especially their use of organic forms in contrast to geometric and mechanical ones.

Georg Jensen's jewelry and silversmithing firm in Copenhagen was the most outstanding exponent of the Scandinavian vernacular style. He operated throughout the postwar period, and his son Soren Georg Jensen continued to maintain his traditions. He employed a number of other well-known designers such as Koppel, Pederson and Malinowski.

—·◆·—

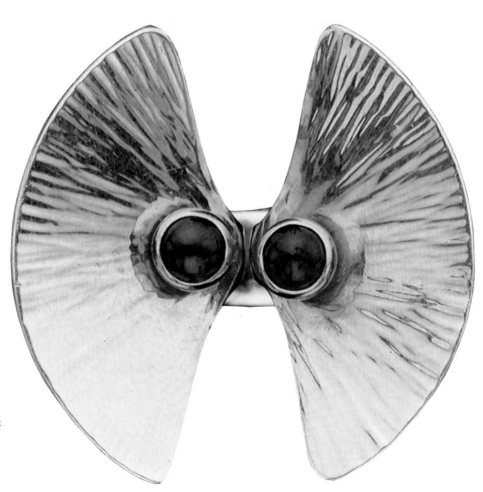

An international abstract ring design by Bent Gabrielson Pederson, who worked for the firm Jensen. c 1960.

The advent of the sixties

It was at the start of the sixties that cheap travel and television heralded the true birth of popular culture. Fashion trends in the early sixties were no longer set by the old guard, but by youth cultures such as the Mods and Rockers, and the Teds. These previously disregarded sectors of society became 'zingos who bolted the pack . . . crashed out of the mould and smashed it to smithereens . . . invented their own look, their own sound, their own age . . . knocked over the establishment and established themselves for today'. (Jody Shields, *All That Glitters*).

The popular image of the sixties is of a society characterized by androgynous fashions, LSD, rock and roll, and women's liberation. While this image has obviously been exaggerated, it has its roots in fact, and the sixties were certainly an era of more youthful and liberal attitudes than previous decades.

A gold and diamond collar, owned by Gloria Vanderbilt. David Webb, 1960.

Early sixties jewelry

Jewelry design inevitably reflected these changing attitudes. Whereas 1950s jewelry had still been divisible into categories of formal and casual wear, these distinctions begin to blur in the 1960s. Jewelry was worn in large quantities. Huge plastic and chunky necklaces were very popular. It was 'hip' for rich and poor not only to wear mini-skirts, but to flaunt fake jewels.

Designers ceased to adhere closely to the dictates of Paris fashion, and instead London became the fashion leader of the period. Mary Quant was the first fashion designer to open a ready-to-wear boutique in London in 1958 with relatively inexpensive clothes and accessories for everyone.

Fashion magazines and films idealized the new style of modern extravaganza. It was favoured by the era's 'first goddess', Jackie Kennedy, which immediately ensured that it would be widely copied, and it held sway from then until the time of the Rolling Stones and The Beatles.

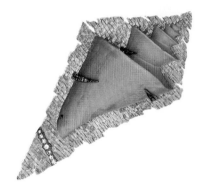

The American jewelry designer, Giorgio di Sant'Angelo was asked by the Du Pont company to make plastic fashion jewelry based on the new Op and Pop Art movements. Kenneth Lane, another costume jeweler working in New York at the time, designed wooden and plastic bangles in snakeskin patterns. He also covered cotton wool Christmas decorations in sequins and enamelled the shells of sea snails.

In addition to new experiments such as these, the sixties saw many reproductions and revivals of old styles, including new-Renaissance, imitation Lalique and Art Deco Cartier.

— · ◆ · —

ABOVE LEFT
—
This brooch with gold and diamonds is typical of the new forms exploited by designers in the sixties, in a move away from the curves of the fifties towards hardness and rock forms. Andrew Grima, Britain, 1960s.

ABOVE RIGHT
—
A collection of jewelry by British designers Frances Beck, Georges Weil, Alan Gard, John Donald, Andrew Grima, Gilian Packard, Geoffrey Turk and Kutchinsky. 1960s.

SIX

Craftsmanship Versus Aesthetics: The Multimedia Form and Function of Jewelry Design

Screen printed polyester
film earrings by Anne
Findly. Edinburgh,
Scotland, 1986–87.

1965–1990

THIS FINAL SECTION EXPLORES the changing function and appearance of international jewelry design over the last 20 years. There is plenty of evidence to show the variety and proliferation of new materials not usually associated with familiar jewelry compositions. In general, there is a desire to move away from the more conservative 'icons of beauty' associated with the high street. Today, individuality, rather than complete identity, is seen as an important visual determinant of personal and artistic expression. For instance, a number of jewelers have been interested in 'making statements' of a political or economic nature, whereas others wish only to explore the possibilities offered by alternative, industrial materials. This offers a chance to experiment and develop ideas outside the decorative arts. However, this has not led, as many have feared, to a decline in techniques. Indeed, many designers continue to work in precious metals and stones, which require the utmost precision and skill. Yet they refuse to be limited by the constraints of trade practice, in terms of aesthetics and the dictates of a market economy.

Eclecticism was the watchword of the sixties. Modern ideas such as Pop Art existed alongside nostalgia (particularly for Art Nouveau and 'flapper' style jewelry). Surface decoration was highly popular, and motifs, often patriotic ones, were inscribed on all varieties of everyday objects. Even the body itself was affected by this trend towards surface decoration, as tattooing came into fashion. At the same time there were many people adhering to the principles of the Arts and Crafts movement, resisting the trend of the old-established jewelers who became ever more commercial in their standards. The organic shapes and uncut crystals of these craft designers are yet another characteristic style of the sixties.

— · ◆ · —

This brooch is an abstract design, in gold, diamond and sapphire, by Georges Weil. During the 1960s he started the Georges Weil Objet d'Art company, which produced sculptures made in precious metals, and his clientele has included H.M. The Queen and Elizabeth Taylor. c 1960.

Aluminium shoulder
pieces and dress
connected, in aluminium
and silk, by Emmy Van
Leersum. Holland, 1967.

In 1969 Neil Armstrong was the first man to walk on the moon, and space-age fashions became a hallmark of the period. Courrèges, the Parisian couturier was the so-called 'godfather of the space-age style', whilst Paco Rabanne remained the major innovator of body jewelry. He used pliers and wires to hinge together circles and squares of plastic into garments.

Jewelry mirrored the futuristic, science fiction trend in many ways. Transparent plastics were widely used. New ideas such as aluminium necklaces-cum-bras were produced. Simple, oversized pieces came into fashion. Metal collars swooped across shoulders. Cardin introduced the enormous industrial zipper and Yves Saint Laurent studded a dress with nailheads, besides producing the chain belt.

The drive towards using new materials was intensified by the soaring prices of gold and platinum in the mid-1960s. As well as new plastics, jewelers experimented with other materials such as titanium. They also looked into new approaches towards form, moving away from the traditional idea of fitting jewelry closely to the body's contours.

—·◆·—

Jewelry as sculpture

The close collaboration between jewelry and the fine arts that had begun in the post-war era continued to have an effect, and in the sixties it was the eye of the sculptor that was brought to bear on traditional views of jewelry. This helped redefine the whole concept of jewelry, blurring the lines of division between its function as a body ornament and its value as an artistic object in its own right. As the decade continued there was a growing distinction between the 'items to wear' type of jewelry made by the conventional trade and 'body sculpture', made by the artist-craftsmen.

Artist-jewelers in Europe and America

The Bauhaus continued to influence art and design establishments throughout Europe, particularly in Britain and Holland, during this period. Designers searched for forms that would be minimalist, universal and democratic. Artists and craftsmen saw themselves as 'pioneers who were liberating the world from the bonds of tradition'. Studio Crafts were established in art schools in America, Australia and Britain. These were small workshops experimenting with alternative jewelry forms.

In Holland, there were debates concerning the value, status and production methods of jewelry made from less precious materials. Jewelers such as Gijs Bakker and Emmy van Leersum sought to bridge the gap between people and their technological, industrial environment. They made objects out of industrial materials such as black rubber and stainless steel, highly crafted and finished to achieve an original effect. Both form and construction were economic. Bakker described the thinking behind his arm bangle, designed to be almost invisible except by the imprint it left on the skin, as follows:

Brooches with different coloured golds and silver by Gilian Packard (top) and John Donald (bottom). These two jewelers were among the first to experiment with contemporary designs for the mainstream 'precious' market. Britain, 1960s.

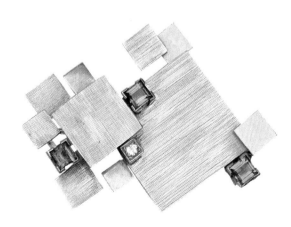

Adam **neckpiece in gilded
brass and PVC laminated
photograph by Gijs
Bakker. Holland, 1988.**

'The imprint has the function of a piece of jewelry. One could call it an organic jewelry piece – organic in the sense that a print is a growing process with a clear course. The wire round the face and the stainless steel circle form around the profile are indications of the very personal face or head. It is just an idea to take away the well-defined function of the face and to let people experience it in another way.' (Peter Dormer and Ralph Turner, *The New Jewelry*)

Germany was as influential as Holland during this period. The centre for the German jewelry trade was still in Pforzheim, with designers such as Hermann Jünger, Reinhold Reiling and Friedrich Becker. In Germany, as in France, the apprenticeship system has remained strong and these three are all respected teachers in the craft. During the 1960s artist-jewelers such as these were encouraging a move towards abstract and conceptual art, seeing their role as being to remain free from the compulsions of industrial production.

In Britain, artist-jewelers, who had been almost non-existent but for Gerda Flöckinger in the 1950s, became very influential during the sixties and have remained so since. British artist-jewelers of the 1960s specialized in informal, contemporary pieces, as epitomized in the work of Andrew Grima. He showed his work at the 1961 exhibition of modern jewelry at the Worshipful Company of Goldsmiths, alongside other jewelers such as Gillian Packard, John Donald and Louis Osman.

In the mid-sixties, a small group of British jewelers, Wendy Ramshaw, David Watkins and Caroline Broadhead, took a new interest in abstraction. In a brief return to the Bauhaus principles of design they gave close consideration to the relationship between form and function. Watkins' work was inevitably influenced by his training as a sculptor. His jewelry pieces are architectonic in form, and stand independently as works of art, rather than being extensions of the person who wears them.

In America, Jean Schlumberger was designing for Tiffany in New York. Following Schiaparelli's work in the thirties, and the 'fantasy' jewelry of the forties and fifties, he experimented with adventurous artistic ideas to break the traditional mould.

—·◆·—

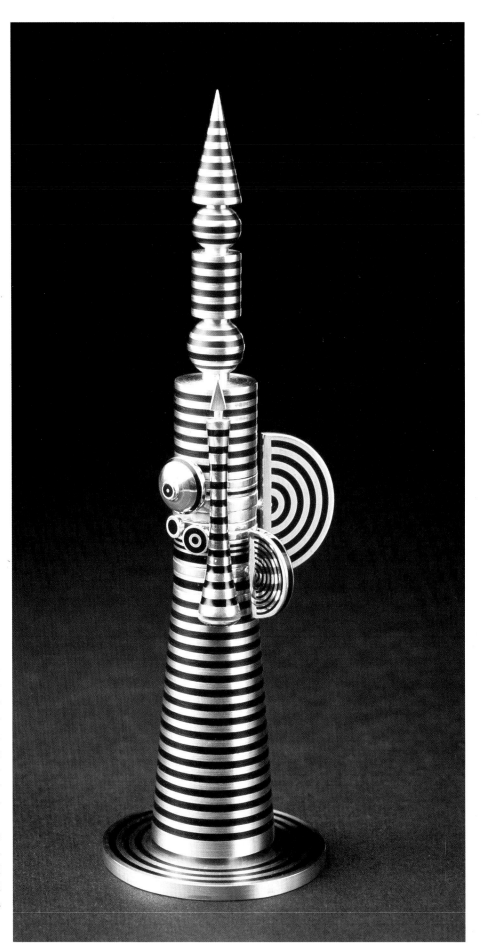

Jewelry for men

It was during the sixties that jewelry first ceased to be perceived as being solely for women. Jody Shields describes the way that the avant-garde idea of jewelry for men percolated through to the fashion market.

'Fashion-conscious men tossed aside neckties in favour of necklaces. With that action, the man on the street joined the ranks of hipster-style revolutionaries like Richard Burton and the Earl of Snowdon. In 1968 the earl wore a gold eagle on a gold chain, plus a copper wrist bracelet. Pierre Cardin offered aluminium and silver pendant necklaces set with uncut diamonds for $1000. In the costume jewelry line, there were necklaces for men dangling disks, bells, abstract shapes, crosses with enamel and fake stones, zodiac symbols and the peace sign. Hippies put ceramic or ivory beads on a ribbon, string, or strip of leather.'

In the music and film industries it became standard practice for men to adorn themselves with a necklace as a symbol of 'more advanced and sensitive states . . . as a counter-cultural gesture' (Jane Mulvagh). This did not always go down well in the trade. Tiffany refused to sell necklaces to men, seeing them as an undesirable sign of effeminacy.

—·◆·—

Pop Art

The plain, bold, geometric style of Pop Art and Op Art which flourished in the 1960s found their way quickly into jewelry design. Clear or black and white constructions were produced in plastic and dyed woods. Man-made materials, particularly moulded plastics such as Plexiglas (ICI Perspex) and vinyl, were prominently used in costume jewelry. Paco Rabanne stamped chainmail shapes out of Perspex, while Charles Jourdan gave his shoes ice-cube shaped Perspex heels, and other decorations in the same material.

Pop Art embraced the highly varied imagery of popular culture. It was in essence anti-functional and ephemeral, reflecting a new ethical code of expendability. The sixties fashion, in direct contrast with today's conservationist trend, was for disposability. Taking up this theme, Rayner Banham said in 1963: 'The aesthetics of pop depend on a massive initial impact and small sustaining powers, and are therefore at their poppiest in products whose sole object is to be consumed.'

The Perspex and paper jewelry made by the British designer, Wendy Ramshaw, in this period were extremely popular and the market was soon saturated with copies of her ideas. She made cheap, disposable paper jewelry which came in kit form, as accessories for paper clothes. Much of it was printed with sixties' ephemera such as Union Jacks, psychedelia and day-glo colours. Ramshaw's own philosophy is that 'any material is viable as long as it is used for the right purposes. For instance, if one works with paper, it is important to accept that it will by its nature, deteriorate and is therefore expendable.'

—·◆·—

Wendy Ramshaw

(BRITAIN, 1939—)

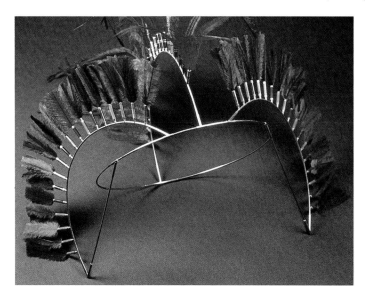

FAR LEFT
—
A Wendy Ramshaw
headpiece in collected
feathers and gold.
England, 1985.

Wendy Ramshaw is an artist-jeweler who has been making jewelry since the late 1960s in a variety of precious and non-precious materials from paper, Perspex and wood to 18ct gold. She has stated recently that:

'I enjoy looking at jewelry and I enjoy wearing jewelry. These are, in simple terms, the real reasons why I am an artist whose main means of expression have become the creation of jewelry.

I make objects whose function it is to decorate the human body and I am also concerned that these items can be enjoyed out of context with the human form, and have at times deliberately devised means by which this can be achieved.'

⟨Wendy Ramshaw in Conversation: Chris Walton⟩

She has always believed that jewelry is a response to the fundamental human need to decorate the body and has often asked questions as regards its function within society, including sexuality, status and custom, alongside its relationship to her own personal development. If this has coincided with contemporary fashion trends, this is mere coincidence rather than intention.

Her jewelry can be worn in a number of different ways. The concept of a set of individual rings all of which can be worn together in various combinations or can be worn separately is carried through to groups of brooches. Her jewelry is designed to be interchangeable and as flexible as possible, to be worn as a 'continually variable and flexible body ornament'.

Her ring sets are particularly interesting because she has exploited features that have been taken for granted. Since the hand is far away from the main frame of the body, it does not always provide an obvious focal point and strong visual impact.

Rings have always been the commonest and 'most loved' form of jewelry that represents eternal love. It is both a message and an ornament and symbolizes the celebration of events such as an engagement or marriage. It may also have other meanings that are expressive of the maker and wearer.

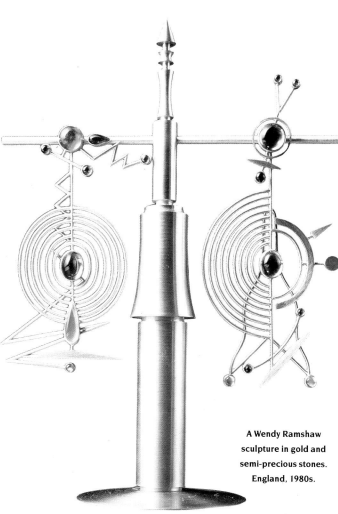

A Wendy Ramshaw
sculpture in gold and
semi-precious stones.
England, 1980s.

RIGHT

RIGHT

Ring sets, in gold and
semi-precious stones, by
Wendy Ramshaw.
England, 1980s.

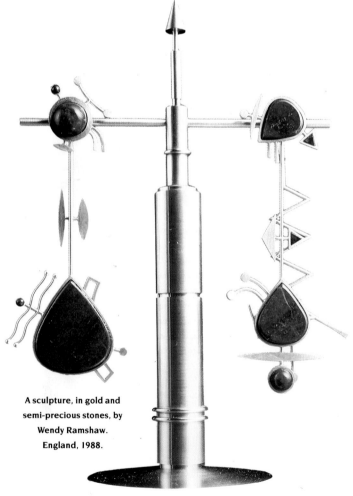

A sculpture, in gold and
semi-precious stones, by
Wendy Ramshaw.
England, 1988.

Picasso's Ladies: More recent examples of Ramshaw's jewelry has been inspired by the abstract qualities inherited from the paintings of the Spanish Cubist, Pablo Picasso. As an artist, he painted in various different guises and was obsessed with women.

These paintings have also provided invaluable source material for Wendy Ramshaw, particularly those which portray characteristic beneficence and sensual poise, such as the portraits of Marie-Therese Walter, who modelled for the artist from 1927. She has deliberately avoided those images of women which are about anger and emotional upheaval. Many of the paintings contain extremely vibrant colours and are deliniated by a complex pattern of black lines. The spiky eyelashes, striped clothing and patterned walls inspired Ramshaw's aesthetic interests.

She has responded to the combination of the formal elements of these paintings, such as the colour, shape, line and volume, with the emotional content inherent within each portrait. She is very much a three-dimensional jeweler whose jewelry reflects similar qualities inherent in the paintings of Picasso. Her own fascination with colour and line has contributed towards the collaboration between the fine and decorative arts. In this instance, the combined associations of painting and jewelry.

It is also possible to detect more formalist elements in her work that originate from the principles of the Modern Movement (such as Constructivism). These theories have influenced the aesthetics of the arts throughout the twentieth century. This is most apparent in Ramshaw's series of ring sets, which when not being worn, are placed back on vertical mounts, thereby resembling miniature sculptures.

Her work is less dependent on traditional craft imagery than other jewelers, possibly because of her training as an illustrator and industrial designer at Newcastle-on-Tyne College of Art. She has also been working with major manufacturers, including Wedgwood. Wendy Ramshaw emphasizes the need for her jewelry to be a starting point, and suggest further possibilities. It is almost as if each piece of material is a word or syllable within a language.

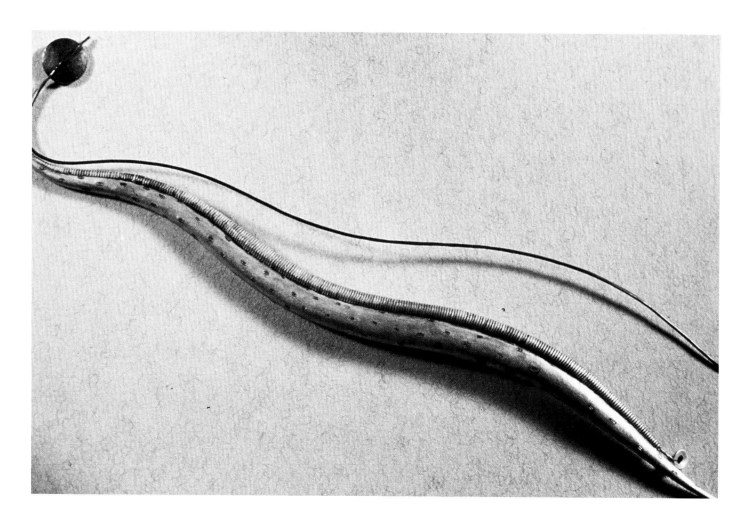

The seventies and eighties

The seventies and eighties have been a period of burgeoning skills and ideas in jewelry making, particularly amongst the artist-jewelers who have continued to flourish and to question the role and nature of jewelry itself. The period has seen the strong promotion of the individual, and the power of street fashion to affect design. Many jewelry designers, such as Watkins, have experimented with new forms and materials, including refractory metals and aluminium, in search of a new artistic language for jewelry. Others, particularly in the cheaper, costume jewelry field, have used their designs more clearly than ever before to express political moods and beliefs.

In the 1970s the cost of the raw materials used in fine jewelry making rose sharply with the deregulation of gold prices. Gold increased from $35 an ounce in the mid-seventies to $850 an ounce by 1981. Sterling silver enjoyed a revival as being relatively

Cynthia Cousens shows such love and concern for her worked metal forms that they take on a living presence. They look like mysterious organic creations that have magically evolved. Silver brooch, England, 1989.

David Watkins started as a sculptor and his concerns with jewelry have been as a sculptural form. Hinged triangle and loop, England, 1975.

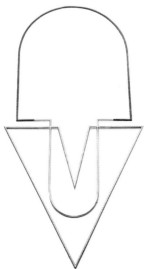

David Watkins' pieces are always precisely conceived and crafted. They can just as easily be hung in a wall-mounted frame as hung around a neck. Hinged loop with triangle and one chevron (neckpiece), England, 1980.

very much cheaper ($2.89 an ounce in 1973) but this was short-lived. With the massive price rise in gold, designers at all levels of the jewelry trade began to look increasingly towards less precious or non-precious materials. This widespread experimentation with alternative materials was clearly illustrated in various exhibitions of the 1970s and 1980s including the following: The Craftsman's Art (Victoria and Albert Museum, London, 1973), The Schmuck International 1900–1980 (Vienna, 1980), Jewelry Redefined (The Crafts Council, London, 1982), The Jewelry Project (The Crafts Council, London, 1983), and The International Jewelry Art Exhibition (Tokyo, 1983).

The last two decades have also been a period of increased international contact and collaboration amongst artist-jewelers. This has played an essential part in the cultivation of new forms and ideas, which have crossed national and cultural boundaries.

ABOVE

Anne Findly's work often shows just how sophisticated plastics can become. Her pieces are tightly controlled and graphic in essence, as with these eminently wearable bangles.

LEFT

These plastic necklaces and bracelets are by Lynn Metcalf. England, 1980s.

— · ◆ · —

Ethnic revivals

During the Flower Power era in the late 1960s and 1970s, the renewed interest in Asia and the Far East led to a return to natural materials such as bone, ivory and Indian metalwork. Western jewelers were influenced by the varied assortment of goods being imported from Asia, and leather thong jewelry hung with dyed feathers and wooden beads typified the ethnic style of this period.

In addition, the 'Black is Beautiful' movement focused attention on African decorative arts. Janis Joplin, the well-known singer and songwriter of the seventies made ethnic jewelry her signature. Men and women pierced their ears to wear hooped earrings.

Anti-Vietnam feeling helped fuel the Peace movement. Patriotic and jingoistic jewelry of the kind produced during and after the Second World War was now replaced with more sentimental motifs, and emotive symbols of peace.

LEFT

Gunilla Treen was one of the pioneer artist/ jewelers to experiment with plastics. Her work in the early seventies excited a lot of people, but upset the traditionalists. Rings, England, 1971–72.

TOP

Landscapes became a popular vehicle for jewelers in the 1970s. Brooches and pendants became like miniature narrative paintings. *Rain* **brooch, Gunilla Treen, 1972.**

Couturiers and jewelry houses took up the Flower Power iconography in a variety of ways. Dior, Chanel, Cartier and Givenchy each had their own version of the jeweled flower.

In keeping with the mood of the time, jewelry was both casual and restrained. It had become chic to reduce ornamentation to a minimum, and was considered vulgar to be too ostentatious. The hand-crafted and ethnic nature of the seventies' jewelry was an expression of anti-materialist values. In this sense it was the jeweler's equivalent of the political slogans that were adorning the fashions of the time.

In Britain, the costume jewelers, Nick Butler and Simon Wilson were particularly influential in the field of reproduction antique jewelry at this time. They revived early twentieth-century Bakelite and paste jewelry.

ABOVE LEFT

Plastics allowed for immediacy and spontaneity in the use of colour, as well as enabling the jeweler to break away from the connotations of elitism and wealth that precious metals and gemstones hold. Brooch, Gunilla Treen, England, 1973.

ABOVE RIGHT

Gunilla Treen made a series of jewelry using laminated plastic sheet with small pieces trapped inside that could slide around, making use of the movements of the wearer. Brooch, England, 1973.

— ◆ —

Street styles and jewelry design

An 18 carat ruby and diamond watch by John Donald. Britain, c 1960.

Pop Art motifs continued to be incorporated into costume jewelry. Mickey Mouse badges had been popularized by the designer Mick Milligan in London, who was commissioned by the fashion designer Zandra Rhodes, to produce accessories for her collections throughout the 1970s. Experiments with cheap materials also continued, and by the mid-eighties the market had been literally saturated with plastic and other non-precious materials.

The liberalizing of attitudes and abandonment of strict codes that had begun in the sixties had led to a general lack of design restraints. High street jewelers went into a frenzy of activity in all sorts of directions. Many used precious materials, even gold, in informal, badly worked and inappropriate ways so they looked like molten lumps. Unsurprisingly, this casual, undisciplined style was not on the whole of interest to the artist-jewelers. However, an exception was John Donald, who did successfully produce some fine jewelry based on this informal street style.

A more widely influential street fashion was the Punk movement which took hold in London in 1977. Punks festooned themselves with so-called 'creative salvage' in the form of safety pins, nuts and bolts, bones, lavatory paper and rubber tyre tubing. The style spread beyond Britain, and for a brief period left its mark on the jewelry market. One jeweler who became closely involved with punk fashion was the Irishman, Tom Binns. He collaborated on a series of Vivienne Westwood's collections in London, including 'Witches and Fluorescent Savages' and 'Punkature'. Setting a trend for jewelry makers to work directly with avant-garde fashion designers, he has also worked with Comme des Garçons and Rifat Ozbek.

From America, a fashion for 'club culture' exotica spread across the Atlantic. This amalgam of styles included rubber fetishist jewelry which was taken up by numerous fashion designers such as Anthony Price and John Galliano.

— ◆ —

Richard Mawdsley

(AMERICA, 1945–)

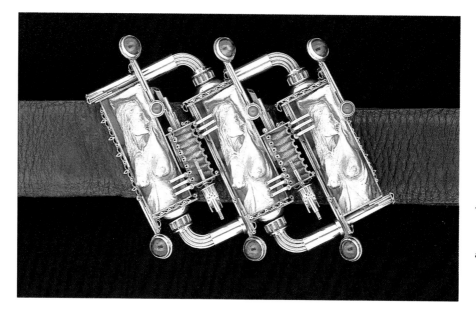

Goneril, Regan, Cordelia. **A buckle made in silver, lapis lazuli and coral. Richard Mawdsley's 'gothic' and machine-like imagery combines with disturbed female forms and, like William Harper, is unencumbered by European design tradition. USA, 1976.**

Much of Richard Mawdsley's work can be found in the form of figurative ornament in many gift shops throughout America. It is instantly accessible because he produces lifelike pieces that look back with nostalgia to the past. The famous Feast Bracelet is particularly well known, because of the detail and craftsmanship applied to it in the form of miniature bottles, fruit and cutlery. It is a virtuoso demonstration of his skills as a jeweler, besides being a well-designed and well-made ornament.

Some of his designs, however, are not as figurative, such as the Medusa pendant or the Goneril, Regan, Cordelia Buckle produced in the late seventies. These pieces have been described as 'Gothic' sculptures and mark a clear distinction between European and American design, particularly in debates concerning the practicality and wearability of jewelry.

Body adornment in America has always been seen as important, possibly because of the lack of tradition in jewelry-making. This has made Americans more open to aspects of jewelry not commonly practised, hence the proliferation of brooches. Brooches do not have to be functional, can be sculptural or decorative and are not generally encumbered by the usual fastenings and other paraphernalia, which may detract from the intended design.

American Indian culture has had a strong influence on jewelry design, personified in the work of a fellow American, William Harper, with the use of organic materials and forms from the thirties. American design has also absorbed the eclectic talents of European émigrés, whose work had often been suppressed by political developments at home. Interestingly, the Bauhaus was reopened in Chicago in 1937, after it had been closed by the Nazis in Germany in 1933.

These factors have had a powerful impact on Mawdsley's designs and their often overwhelming effect on the wearer. He is also committed to producing functional designs, although they are often very heavy and dominating constructions.

Susanna Heron

(BRITAIN, 1949—)

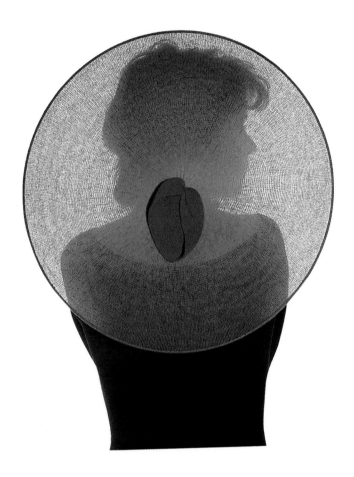

A large turquoise and
red hat developed from
Susanna Heron's
'Wearables' collection,
which explores the
relationship between
sculpture and the human
form. Britain, 1982.

Susanna Heron has proved to be a successful exponent of body jewelry or jewelry as miniature sculpture, a concept developed in America and Holland.

Along with Caroline Broadhead, her work stands out as having made a significant contribution towards re-evaluating the traditional concept of jewelry. From the mid-seventies, she began producing a collection of acrylic Perspex bangles. Her work has explored geometry and colour in ornament, which has developed into 'wearables', not unlike familiar clothing types. These were made to hang on walls and not to wear.

Heron's work in recent years has moved towards sculptural metaphor, where the exact meaning of her work is not clearly understood. There is an obvious fascination with exploiting the qualities inherent in the decorative arts and blurring the distinctions between art and craft.

British artist-jewelers

Artist-jewelers in Britain in the seventies gained two new means by which to promote their work. One was the opening of an important retail outlet, Electrum, in London. The other was the establishment of the Crafts Advisory Committee, later renamed the Crafts Council. This was set up in 1971 to promote and develop the importance of British crafts. Before this, jewelers had had to rely on editorials in fashion magazines such as *Honey, Vogue* and *Harpers and Queen* to publicize their work.

Daphne Kriṇos has the knack of making a little say a lot. Her delicate and elegant pieces are always intriguing, with her subtle use of line and eye-catching sparks of colour, like the cube of gold. Brooch, England, 1989.

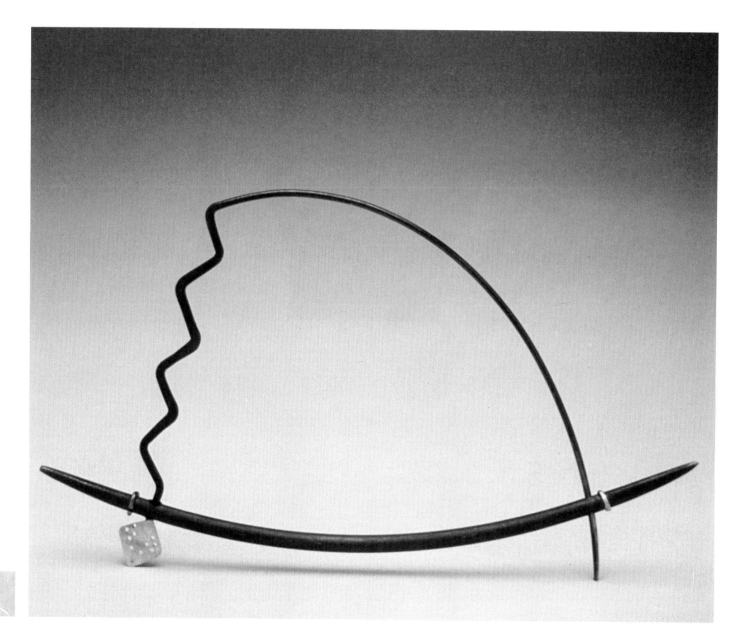

Sometimes the political message within contemporary jewelry designs has been made more explicit. For instance, David The British artist-jewelers concentrated on simple, handmade pieces based on the Scandinavian craft tradition. They used newly devised techniques and took advantage of the influx of bright new synthetic materials. Some craft jewelers felt that the crude settings of rocky stones in precious metals produced for the high street outlets represented an unacceptable adherence to commercial values and hierarchical dogma. Their own hand-crafted pieces deliberately set out to counteract this ethos.

'Urban Ethnic' is an apt title for this controlled evocation of primitive forms and symbols. Earrings, Daphne Krinos, England, 1989.

Poston protested against the poor working conditions and exploitation of black miners in South Africa by exhibiting a forged steel neckpiece in the shape of a manacle. Inlaid in silver were the words 'diamonds, gold and slavery for ever'.

Many artist-jewelers in recent decades have wanted to cross the barrier between the connoisseur and the general markets, to make their jewelry more widely accessible. However, this is not easily done as art jewelry can often not be translated into a form that can be mass-produced without seriously compromising the design. Some individuals, such as Ramshaw, have found a halfway house by designing limited editions of their work commissioned for sale by museums.

TOP LEFT

Ann Marie Shillito was one of the first jewelers to use the refractory metals of niobium and titanium. Developed initially for the aerospace industry, they were soon discovered by jewelry designers. Brooch, Edinburgh, Scotland, 1989.

BOTTOM LEFT

This lovely curving fibula shows Ann Marie Shillito's concern for a 'complete' design, that does not have need of extraneous fixtures to attach it to the wearer's clothing. Edinburgh, Scotland, 1986.

Titanium's wonderful colour properties, lightweight and tough, non-corrosive surface, make it an ideal material for both the fashion jeweler and the more exacting artist/jeweler. Brooches, Ann Marie Shillito, Edinburgh, Scotland, 1989.

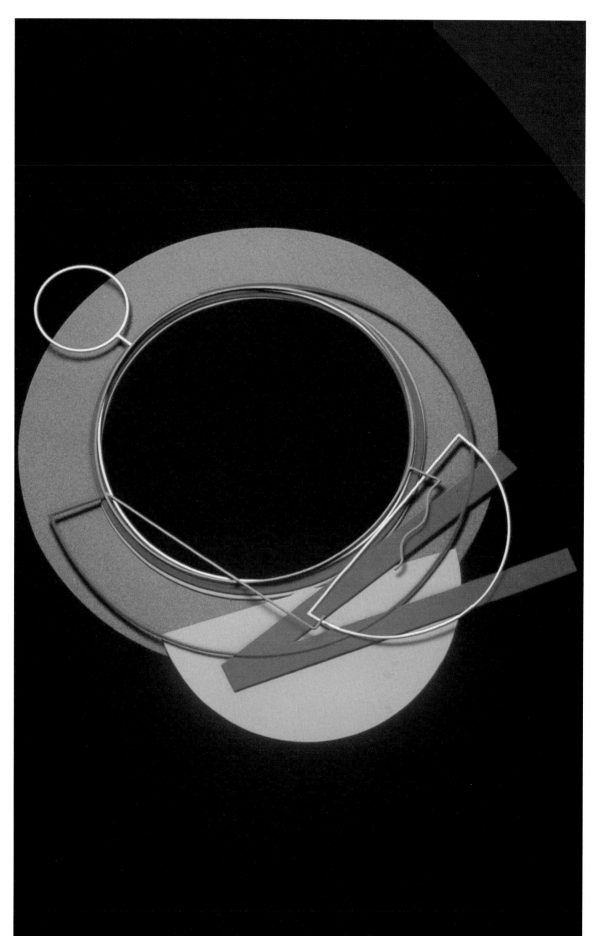

David Watkins' more recent work has become very two-dimensional, colour and line taking over from sculptural form. Necklace, England, 1980s.

David Watkins has concentrated on non-political 'body forms'. He insists that his work is not jewelry as such. The forms he designs have to be appreciated spatially, as well as in relation to the body. Supple organic shapes contrast with rigid Perspex to complement the body's outline. His pieces range from the very simple to more elaborate and theatrical celebrations of technology.

The classical style of the Bauhaus continued to have an influence into the early eighties. British jewelers such as Ramshaw, Jöel Degen, Eric Spiller and David Watkins have applied the Bauhaus notion of the machine aesthetic. As Ramshaw has pointed out:

'We are here in the presence of a machine, not a craft aesthetic, though much craft is involved in the making and the machinery is closely controlled by the designer-craftsman. Mass-production should not be looked down upon as a debased form of manufacture, as long as the object is well made. An excellent finish is often only achieved by using mass-production techniques because of the high cost of "tooling up".'

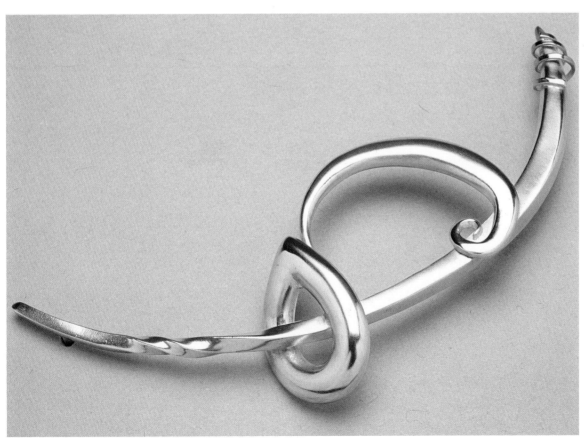

TOP LEFT
—
Iron silver ring by Susan May. England, 1983.

BOTTOM LEFT
—
Brooch by Susan May in iron silver and gold. England, 1984.

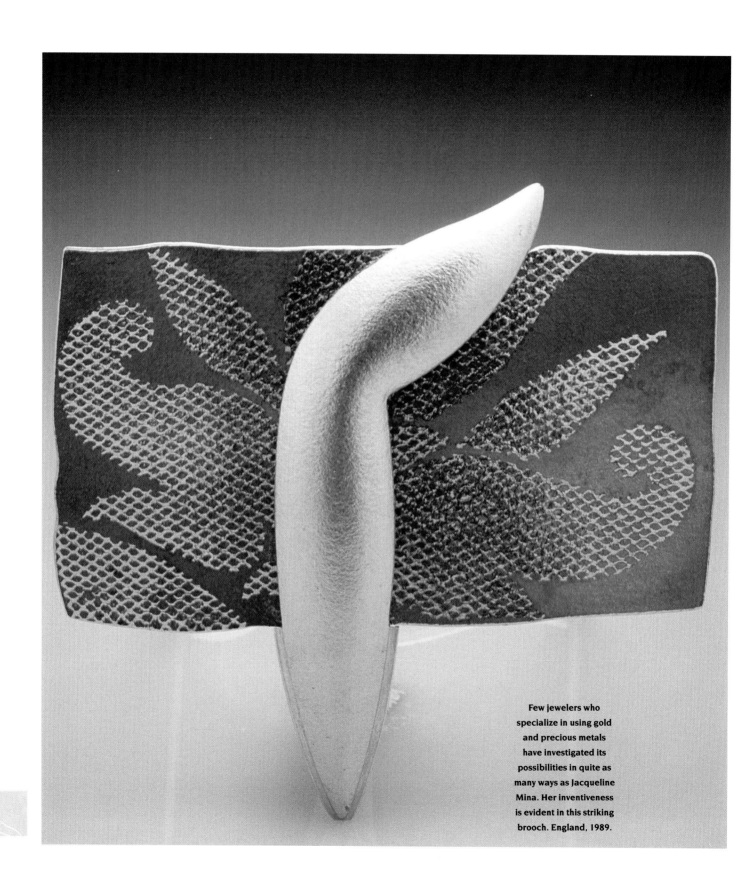

Few jewelers who specialize in using gold and precious metals have investigated its possibilities in quite as many ways as Jacqueline Mina. Her inventiveness is evident in this striking brooch. England, 1989.

Some modern jewelry design has encroached onto the territory of clothing. The British designer, Susanna Heron, for example, produced a series of designs called 'wearables', which were transparent layered collars. When not in use they were intended to hang on the wall as a sculptural form.

Other designers such as Nuala Jamison, Julia Manheim and Caroline Broadhead have continued to explore the use of colour transparency and synthetic materials.

LEFT
—
Silver and gold granulation rings by Dorothy Hogg. England, 1972.

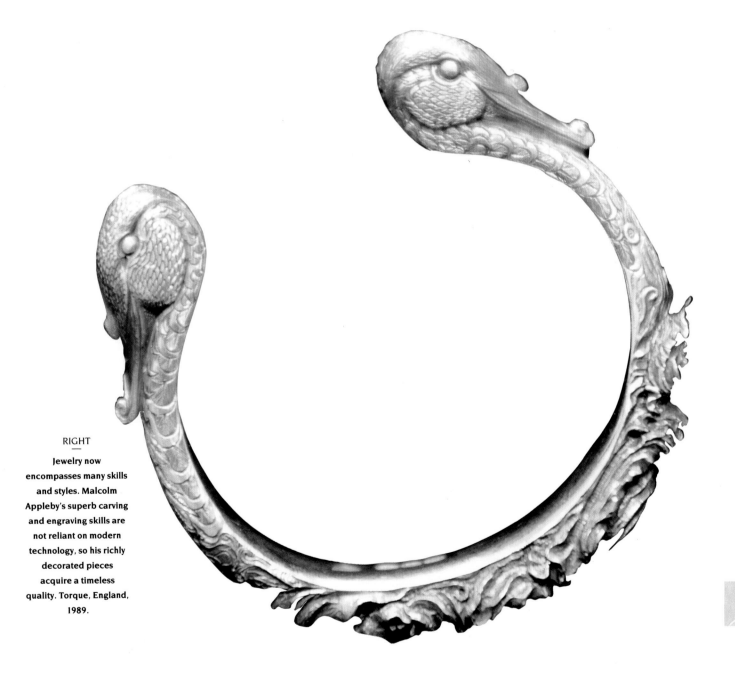

RIGHT
—
Jewelry now encompasses many skills and styles. Malcolm Appleby's superb carving and engraving skills are not reliant on modern technology, so his richly decorated pieces acquire a timeless quality. Torque, England, 1989.

Ring, bracelet, brooch
and earrings in injection-
moulded plastic by
Simon Costin. England,
1989.

Earrings, in oxidized
metals, by William
Gilbert. England, 1989.

A recent Royal College of Art graduate who is interested in the 'intellectual' aspects of conceptual jewelry is Simon Fraser. He says of himself that he 'sometimes makes jewelry and sometimes makes something like jewelry'. His work marries together emotional and intellectual elements, and is influenced in particular by three diverse themes: performance art (especially the work of Rose English in contemporary theatre), current political issues, and micro-organisms. Much of Fraser's work is made from alternative materials such as injection-moulded plastics and foodstuffs (for example, necklaces made of dog biscuits). He rather glibly remarks that he has 'always wanted (his) jewelry to get drunk, have rows, go to parties and fall downstairs'.

— · ◆ · —

David Watkins

(BRITAIN, 1940–)

A large turquoise and red hat developed from Susanna Heron's 'Wearables' collection, which explores the relationship between sculpture and the human form. Britain, 1982.

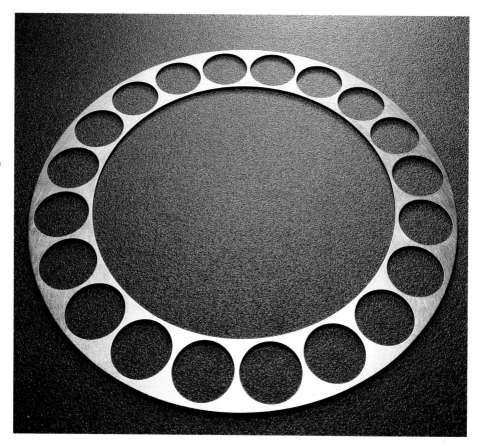

BELOW
—
David Watkins' *Blue Dancer* neckpiece in paper, steel and ink. England, 1983.

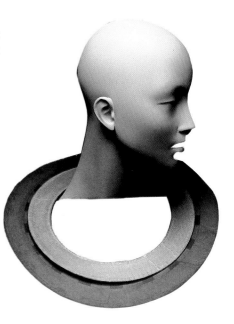

Watkins is a jeweler, metalworker and sculptor concerned about both the relationship between his work and its environment and the intrinsic nature of the piece itself.

A more recent selection of his work includes a series of collar designs in materials such as titanium, gilded brass, neoprene and color-core. Watkins often uses colours that we associate with metal in glossy or matt finishes.

Many of his neckpieces are large and circular and geometric in design, lightweight and therefore easy to wear. They are simple, finely executed designs. The ornamentation for these pieces has been worked out with the use of computer-aided technology. This has been an invaluable tool that has enabled the designer to try out new designs and sizes without the need to waste materials, as well as saving time.

These neckpieces act as both sculpture and jewelry. They exist to conjure up images of the future and this is emphasized further by the names he uses to identify these images, such as Voyager and Emerald Outrigger. Watkins is also fascinated with the organic (botanical and zoological) nature of these pieces and the magical qualities associated with ancient cultures and architectonic forms.

His work can be worn or displayed on the wall, for their circular form is suggestive of the neck they embrace, the face they reflect: even perhaps a hollow mask. Watkins is discovering the importance of shapes and their relationship to their environment and finding new ways of 'making less mean more'.

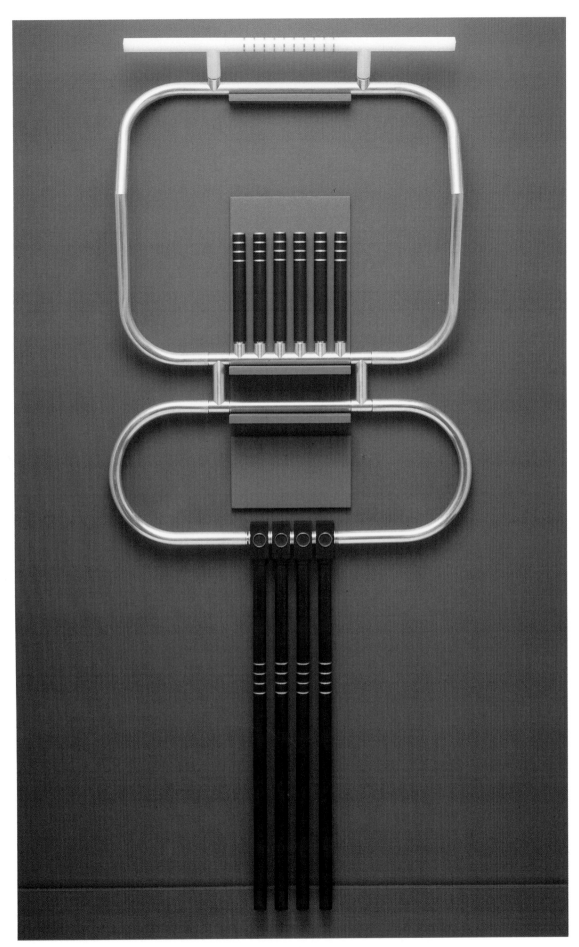

A large pendant
bodypiece, in acrylic, 18
carat gold and
aluminium, by David
Watkins. England, 1975.

Julia Manheim

(BRITAIN, 1949—)

Julia Manheim has been exploring the ideas behind body sculpture, whereby jewelry can be seen as an expressive extension of clothing design. She is particularly interested in jewelry as a reflection of social and economic patterns and believes that as a medium, jewelry acts as a shell or mask under which the sensitive can feel courageous and confident. In terms of design, some of her work appears in direct contrast to the wealth and status associated with the wearing of gold jewelry, because the emphasis is placed on the individual and his or her relationship to other objects in the environment.

Other designers have also explored this close relationship between jewelry and clothing, such as Caroline Broadhead and Pierre Degen. They also believe that clothing and jewelry can act as a mask through which we project ourselves.

During the early 1980s, this has paralleled similar developments in the Haute Couture industry. For example, Manheim maintains a powerful sense of the individual in the utilization of steel and plastic frames. These pieces are similar to the sculptural forms executed by the Japanese fashion designer, Issey Miyake.

Manheim's work concentrates on large volumes and abstract shapes. She tends to use very harsh colours which reflect her experience of working in the industrial heartland of Newcastle in northeast England. Her tabard and cloak designs are very bold and represent a psychological suit of armour against twentieth-century conformity and tradition. Alongside these designs, she has also become interested in a linear range of work based on the ladder. She employs plastic-coated steel wire, put together on full figures and busts. They emphasize the importance of the body in relation to these pieces of body sculpture.

Slatted body cages offer neither comfort nor conformity. They express a very bizarre way of dressing, indicating that the rib cage should be worn outside the body. They may even introduce an element of discomfort to the viewer. These ideas are a direct attack on conventional codes of dress. Her figures bend and twist in outline forms, to complement the delicacy and quality of the work itself. These cages are a direct response to her seeing a man carrying a ladder, by slotting it over his shoulders. It is a metaphor which suggests perhaps the impact of external, usually unconscious forces within a social environment upon the expressiveness of the individual.

Jewelry is seen in this instance as a positive expression which criticizes the precarious achievements of mankind.

LEFT

Two peaks bracelet in printed paper by Julia Manheim. England, 1985.

RIGHT

Julia Manheim's Greek-loaf armpieces in painted paper. England, 1985.

Jane Adam

(BRITAIN, 1959—)

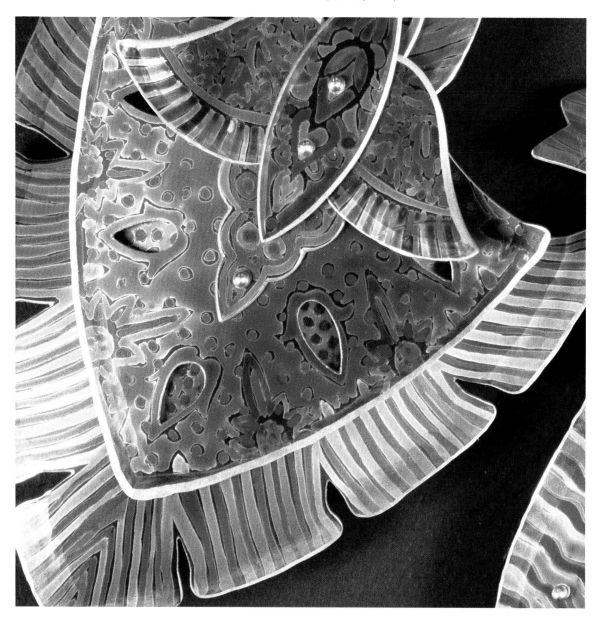

LEFT
—
Jane Adam brooches,
with layers of dyed and
anodized aluminium.
England, 1989.

RIGHT
—
Brooches and earrings
by Jane Adam in
anodized aluminium.
England, 1988.

Jane Adam utilizes the versatile qualities of anodized aluminium, which can be painted, dyed or printed in much the same way as textile or paper-making techniques. However, being a metal, it is hard and durable and can be shaped into more permanent three-dimensional forms.

Anodized aluminium involves the process of electro-chemical techniques. This gives the metal a hard, transparent layer of aluminium oxide, which, although colourless, can absorb special dyes and inks. These colours are chemically sealed into the surface and cannot chip or flake off.

Adam's work explores the application of colour, and the techniques which she uses are of her own invention. Some of her most recent work has involved printing with coloured inks, applied with rubber stamps.

David Hensel

(BRITAIN, 1945–)

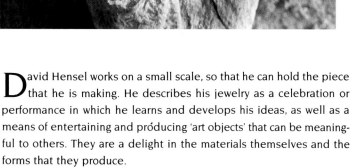

David Hensel works on a small scale, so that he can hold the piece that he is making. He describes his jewelry as a celebration or performance in which he learns and develops his ideas, as well as a means of entertaining and próducing 'art objects' that can be meaningful to others. They are a delight in the materials themselves and the forms that they produce.

He explains that the world is full both of people and their images. In effect, this produces an overlap between reality and construction. Hensel develops these ideas by layering, and through surface details of contrasts and multiple expressions, masked and helmeted people, erosion and fragmentation inherent in 'antiquities and sea-worn things', combinations of found objects with carefully made ones.

The size of these pieces is important, because although they remain relatively small, they create an illusion of immensity. They cross the boundary between sculpture and jewelry. They act as a reflection of this double-sided world, as adornment and as objects of contemplation.

ABOVE

A pendant in carved quartz crystal, ivory, gold and opals. David Hensel, England, 1988.

FAR LEFT

A David Hensel pendant in ebony, ivory, opals, gold, pearl and silver. England, 1987.

Kim Ellwood

(BRITAIN, 1956—)

K im Ellwood's jewelry is constructed essentially from steel and combined with coloured, industrial base enamels and gold leaf. She enjoys the strength and intractibility found in the steel medium. The metallurgical qualities inherent in this material can produce beautiful subtleties of colour in the oxidation process. This is enhanced when colours are developed chemically and contrasts powerfully with her use of very bright enamels and gold embellishments.

Her work is an exploration in the abstraction of figures and armour and the ancient symbolism attached to spirals, crescents and arches, as well as her enthusiasm for stripes. Some of Ellwood's earlier pieces explored the medium of tin, which she discovered in the construction of tin toys. She describes these brooches and earrings as naive in character and of simple construction.

Brooches in steel and enamel by Kim Ellwood. England, 1989.

Germany and Holland

In Germany, mixed media imagery has been exploited by jewelers such as Gerd Rothman and Ulrike Bahrs, while Claus Bury's work has manifested conceptual forms. Bahrs' designs range from intricate gold pendants and brooches to pins that incorporate rubber thread. His work has been characterized as being rather ambiguous, and narrow in its range of ideas. However, Peter Dormer and Ralph Turner have pointed out in *The New Jewelry* that 'such jewelers, like sculptors, sometimes have over-optimistic expectations that people will make the correct deductions about the specific meaning of their work'.

In Holland, Leersum and Bakker turned the very notion of jewelry on its head when they experimented with simple forms that were both clothing and jewelry.

— · ◆ · —

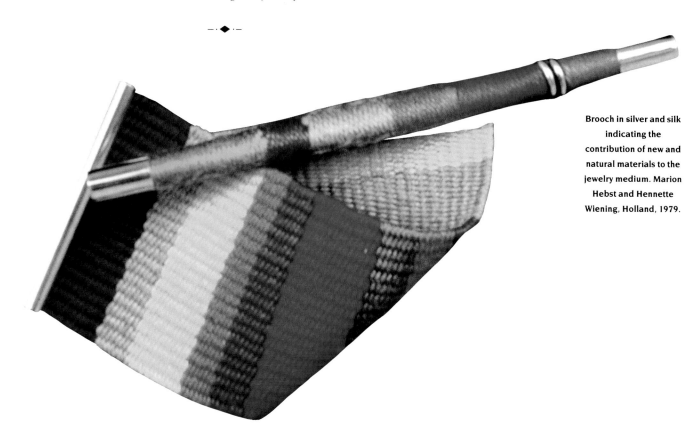

Brooch in silver and silk indicating the contribution of new and natural materials to the jewelry medium. Marion Hebst and Hennette Wiening, Holland, 1979.

Gijs Bakker's *One page
newspaper* **neckpiece,
paper coated in PVC.
Holland, 1983.**

Emmy van Leersum   Gijs Bakker

(HOLLAND, 1930–1984)   (HOLLAND, 1942–)

Bracelet in 14 carat gold
by Emmy Van Leersum.
Holland, 1979.

During the sixties and early seventies, new radical departures have been made in the jewelry field. In Holland, Emmy van Leersum and Gijs Bakker reacted against the traditional use of precious materials and the connotations associated with this, such as exclusiveness and wealth. Both designers exploited the use of familiar industrial materials such as steel, black rubber and aluminium. This was considered to be an unusual practice at the time. They also used the whole body as a potential canvas upon which to place their pieces.

The impression made on the skin by the use of tight wire arm bracelets or the use of crude cylindrical forms were metaphors for our current preconceptions about jewelry and its relationship to the body.

Jewelry in Holland tended to develop more rapidly because of the current trends within art and design and its close associations with precision manufacture and high technology. However, many of their designs were highly crafted pieces and finished in such a way as to suggest a hi-tech background to the designs.

Van Leersum and Bakker developed very clear ideas about the changing role of the jewelry medium at this time. Their minimalist and democratic approach to design was extremely influential in the formation of a national style.

Van Leersum describes the process of designing her bracelets as being one in which she wishes to 'dismantle all the old conventions and start afresh, from the beginning: there is the human arm and it needs covering. An arm has, roughly, the shape of a cylinder, so I took standard cylinders as my basic form'.

‹New Tradition, The Evolution of Jewellery: Caroline Broadhead›

Wilhelm Mattar

(WEST GERMANY, 1946–)

Architectural principles and forms are echoed in the works of Wilhelm Mattar. His work is monumental by virtue of the elegance of the volumes, which seem to be defined alongside architectural forms. His use of granite, concrete and gold as materials reinforces their effect of monumentality which transcends their scale and function as jewelry.

Brooch, in mother of pearl and gold plated, by Wilhelm Mattar. West Germany, 1989.

Australia

Australian jewelry design has benefited from the intimate collaboration between artist-craftsmen on an international basis in recent years. Many European designers have travelled to Australia, conducting workshops and exhibiting their work, and a number of innovative Australian designers have emerged from this initial contact. Helge Larsen, Peter Tully, Rowena Gough, Dirani Lewers and Jenny Toynbee, some of whom have trained in Germany, are foremost amongst them.

— · ◆ · —

A Lam de Woolf neckpiece. 'Wearables' made of wood and painted textiles, concerned with the relationship between body and sculptural forms. Holland, 1980s.

America

An important development for artist-jewelers in America was the opening of the specialist retail outlet, Sculpture to Wear (later Artwear) in New York. American designers in the seventies were less concerned than their European counterparts with traditional constraints. The work of designers such as Richard Mawdsley, Robert Ebendorf, William Harper and Mary Lee Hu is more art form than jewelry. It illustrates the extent to which the old barriers between different design disciplines

The *Temptation of St Anthony* **in gold cloisonne enamel on silver. This piece reflects William Harper's interest in a diverse range of tribal cultures within North America. USA, 1960s.**

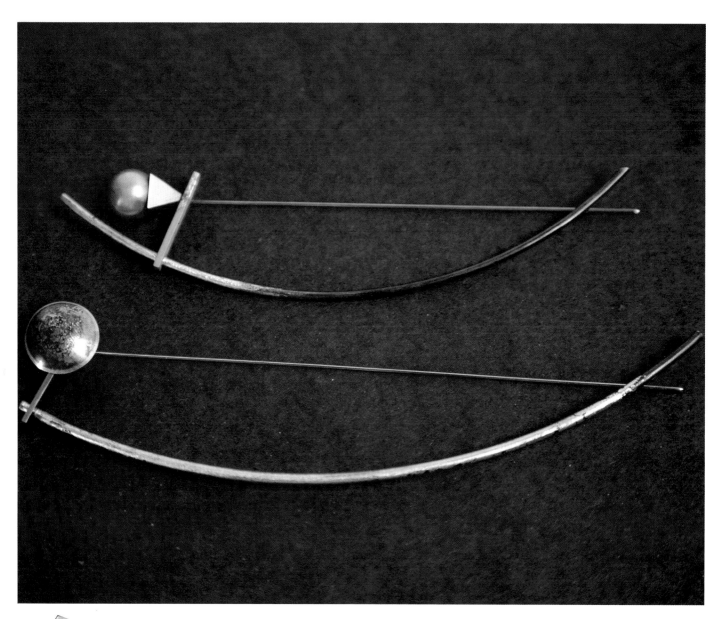

ABOVE

The fine lines and curves
in these brooches
present a delicate
balance and harmony,
perhaps reflecting Trevor
Jennings interest in
Japan and the East. They
are contemplative forms
rather than mere
decoration. England,
1989.

ABOVE

Trevor Jennings is a
master of under-
statement. His exquisite
use of metals in simple,
sparing forms shows a
cool perfection – and
then a hint of humour,
like the twist in the tail of
this pin. England, 1989.

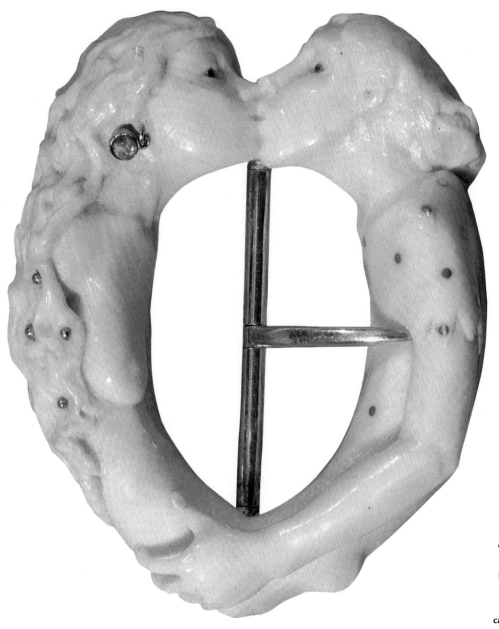

David Hensel's richly carved pieces seem to relate to folklore and history. They are more 'vernacular' than sculptural; his skilful carvings work directly on the nostalgic emotions. Belt buckle, England, 1978.

Susan Barr has embraced the 1980s passion for combining images from different ages and cultures with engaging results. *Bird on a Pillar* **and** *Back to the Square* **brooches, England, 1980s.**

had broken down by the 1970s. These designers drew on American Indian Art, assemblage art and abstract expressionism.

The designers who exhibited at Artwear were constantly approached by fashion designers for their work. However their pieces cannot be considered to be costume jewelry as such. The criterion for having them included in the Artwear gallery was that 'the artists pioneered the art of jewelry making, using materials in an unexpected and novel manner.'

That ideal sums up the new creative spirit that has entered jewelry design in the twentieth century. Of course, companies such as Cartier, Asprey, Garrard and Tiffany are still producing time-honoured designs using precious metals and gemstones. These pieces represent traditional values, which will always retain an importance, and they offer secure investments for the future. However, it is in the work of artist-jewelers such as those described in this chapter that we find the expression of the new ideas and new attitudes towards jewelry that have arisen during the course of this century. It is in this sphere of jewelry design that the boundaries of modern inventiveness and contemporary social comment will continue to be extended.

— . ◆ . —

Kevin Coates

(BRITAIN, 1950–)

Caliban. **A ring in carved grey moonstone, inlaid rubies and yellow gold. Kevin Coates, England, 1985.**

Kevin Coates would describe his 'figurative' work, not only as a literal use of imagery, but as figurative elements within an abstracted context. Each of his pieces is characterized by a spiritual symbolism that is integral to the design. He sees jewelry as talisman, in that it has a power that is unique to wearer and owner, and that it may harness the opposing energies of concept and visual form, objectivity with emotional expression.

He has pointed out that:

'Through sign, symbol, and meaning, images themselves become embodiments of energy, which is one reason why they present such difficulties in use, for whilst there is an acknowledged, accepted, visual language of meaning, there is, too, that corresponding, unpredictable web, which is the viewer's experience, woven between the meaning intended, and the meaning comprehended . . .'

It is this 'poetic association' which Coates believes serves the jeweler's art more than any other. Our worldly obsession with the intrinsic value of materials has impoverished our aesthetic and spiritual sensibilities. He suggests that this is also the reason that so many contemporary jewelers have become contemptuous of such luxury and have, instead, moved on to use 'new' materials.

As a goldsmith, however, he has found it a useful vehicle of expression, through form, colour, rhythm and proportion. His work is essentially a slow process in which a 'journey from unconscious to concious thought' is made.

David Laplantz

(AMERICA, 1944–)

David Laplantz is described as a 'limited production jeweler' and is currently Professor of Art at the Humboldt State University, Arcata, California.

He incorporates a variety of traditional, as well as new, materials, such as coloured and anodized aluminium, lizard skins and egg-crate plex, besides anything else which expresses his sense of humour and design in a wearable art form.

For many years, he has made innumerable objects from toys to piggy banks, but always wanted to be a 'real' jeweler. Since the 1980s, he has been working in the anodizing and colouring of aluminium, in order to 'play out living dreams in anodized technicolor'.

His work has been described as spontaneous, miniature art forms, which stand out on their own when not being worn. He is apparently instinctive and characterizes 'the epitome of an American ideal which manages to combine competitiveness, ambition, ego and energy in the belief that life should be lived with wholesome enjoyment . . .'

David Laplantz has achieved rapid importance in the world of contemporary American jewelry, because of his speed in design and manufacture. His most recent work has included the use of neon, which has developed from a project for an Arch Neon Wall Piece. His interest in jewelry results from the intimacy he feels can be achieved from this medium. He says that, 'there is something nice about the precious metals, gold and silver, and the less-than-noble metals of copper, brass, bronze and aluminium.'

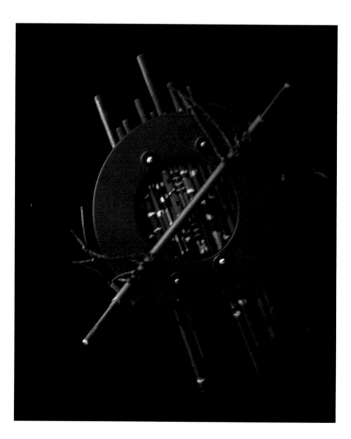

RIGHT
—
A David Laplantz
bracelet. California,
USA, 1983/4.

BELOW LEFT
—
A David Laplantz brooch.
California, USA, 1985.

Giampaolo Babetto

(ITALY, 1947–)

Giampaolo Babetto's work is both classical and 'chic'. He works in gold because of its universal applicability. It possesses the qualities of ductility and elegance and he often combines this metal with other materials, contrasting it in colour and structure.

His pieces are seldom solid forms, but rather hollow three-dimensional items that are perfectly constructed out of curved or plane sheets which are then welded or soldered into seemingly solid forms.

Babetto is certainly a minimalist jeweler, whose work compares favourably with Emmy van Leersum and Gijs Bakker in Holland. For all its reductivist and purist qualities, his work is by no means devoid of aesthetic expression.

— · ◆ · —

Hermann Jünger

(WEST GERMANY, 1928–)

German jewelry design in the last 30 years has contributed significantly towards modern jewelry design. Notable amongst key designers during this period are Friedrich Becker, Reinhold Reiling and Hermann Jünger.

Hermann Jünger is a fine goldsmith, who has developed aesthetic and technical awareness within the jewelry industry since the sixties. His teaching as Professor at the Academy of Fine Arts in Munich has influenced a number of artist-craftsmen now working in Europe, America and Australia, such as Daniel Kruger (USA), Miriam Sharlin (USA) and Otto Kunzli (West Germany).

He has worked extensively in kinetic jewelry, which reflects the relationship between motion and jewelry forms. He uses drawing to discover new ideas and capture a spontaneity that would be difficult to produce in the jewelry-making process itself. Ostensibly, he is influenced by the German painter, Julius Bissier, whose Oriental compositions conveyed an emotional and psychological attitude that attracted Jünger.

Jünger is certainly inspired by the legacy of the Bauhaus, in keeping the design elements to a minimum, whilst simultaneously incorporating a more experimental approach and exploration of the intrinsic qualities of materials. This has parallels with the teachings of the Preliminary Course initiated at the Bauhaus in the 1920s.

Jünger has continued to employ a variety of different shapes and images within the traditional jewelry vocabulary, which has an affinity with natural and found objects.

Lisa Gralnick

(AMERICA)

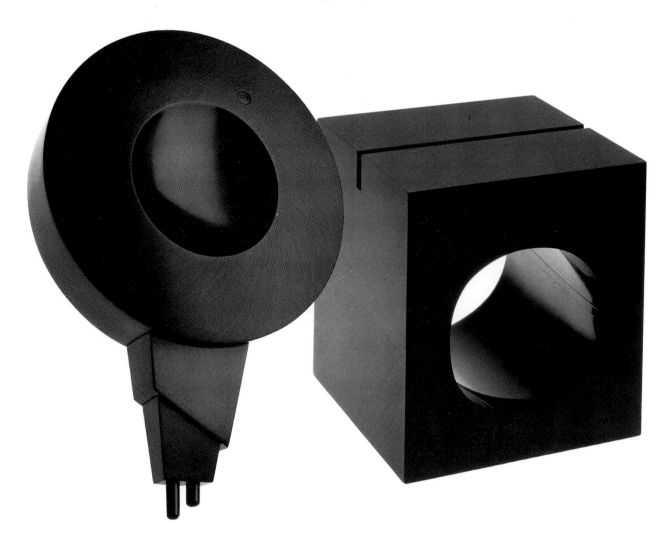

ABOVE LEFT

Brooch in black acrylic
by Lisa Gralnick, a subtle
political commentator of
the late eighties. New
York, USA, 1988.

ABOVE RIGHT

Bracelet in black acrylic
by Lisa Gralnick. New
York, USA, 1988.

Today, Lisa Gralnick's work is characterized by the distinctive black jewelry which she has produced from thin, lightweight and flat acrylic sheets. This has resulted from many years of working in precious materials and being unable to communicate a changing vision of the world within the confines of traditional goldsmithing work.

Increasingly, Gralnick has become obsessed with dark and rather threatening forms, such as submarines and missiles. These she feels are seemingly tragic in their beauty and ironic in their associations with a mundane world, and her jewelry expresses this relationship between human frailty and a decaying post-industrial society.

This work has the appearance of solid castings or having been carved directly from material such as ebony. The density of these pieces are surprising in their seeming weightlessness. Their forms are regular geometric shapes, constructed from triangles, discs and rectangles.

Underlying themes in her work include architectural references to houses, obelisks and simple monuments and marine imagery in the form of boat keels or submarine hulls.

A

Adam, Jane, 108
Aga Khan, 40
American Crafts Council, 63
American Free Dress League, 23
American Indian art, 29, 92, 120
Appleby, Malcolm, 101
architecture, 12, 29, 115
  Bauhaus, the, 54, 63, 70
  Chicago School of Design, 54
  Moholy-Nagy, Lazlo, 54, 63
Arden, Elizabeth, 68
Arp, Jean, 47–8
Art Deco, 27–38, 56
  artist-jewelers, 35
  bangle, 37
  bracelet, 34
  Chanin Building, 29
  Chrysler Building, 29
  Cleopatra look, 29
  Lacloche, 27, 55
  necklace, 30
  pendant, 30
  plastic, use of, 43
  style, 29
  wrist-watch, 34
Artificers Guild, 16
artist-jewelers, 35, 70–2, 80, 94–6, 117, 120
Art Nouveau, 11–13, 40, 78
  in Britain, 14–17
  in Europe, 14
  in France, 25, 27
Arts and Crafts movement (UK), 8, 12, 14–16, 19, 23–4, 78
Arts and Crafts movement (US), 24
Artwear (NY), 117, 120
Ashbee, C R, 15, 16, 25
Aspreys, 7, 62, 120
Australia, 116
Austria, 21

B

Babetto, Giampaola, 124
Bahrs, Ulrike, 112
Baker, Oliver, 14, 23
Bakker, Gijs, 80–1, 112–114, 124
Ballet Russes, 37, 39–40
bangles, 34, 48
  Art Deco, 37
  Boucheron, 58
  Perspex, 93
  plastic, 88
  'slave', 48
  snakeskin, 75
  wooden, 75
barbaric style, 34
Barr, Susan, 6, 120
Bauhaus, the, 54, 60, 63, 70, 80, 82, 92, 99, 124
Becker, Friedrich, 82, 124
belts, 14, 23
  buckles, 14, 16, 23, 92, 119
  thirties, 36
Berklander, George, F, 43
Berlin iron jewelry, 52
Bernhardt, Sarah, 11, 13, 22
Bing, Samuel, 13
Binns, Tom, 9
Bissier, Julius, 124
Boivin, Rene, 40
boquet jewelry, 46
Boucheron, 7, 13, 33, 55–6
  bangle, 58
Bowles, Janet Payne, 24
bracelets, 11, 32, 34
  ankle, 68
  arabesque, 60
  Cartier, 40, 46
  charm, 68
  copper, 83
  Danish, 53
  feast, 92
  gold, 114

Goldfinger, 58
Gralnick, 125
Har, 60
Laplantz, 122–3
Leersum, 114
Mazer, 59
paper, 106
plastic, 35, 88
two peaks, 106
Braque, Georges, 30–1, 48, 58, 60–1
Britain Can Make It, 52
Broadhead, Caroline, 82, 93, 101, 106, 114
brooches, 17, 19, 21, 28
  anodized aluminium, 108
  anthropomorphic, 60
  Art Deco, 41
  Barr, 120
  boat and insect, 54
  Boucheron, 56
  cactus, 51
  diamond and tourmaline, 22
  dragon, 69
  enamel, 111
  forties palm, 54
  Gralnick, 125
  Haskell, 66
  Jennings, 118
  jester, 57
  Krinos, 94
  Lacloche, 55
  ladybird, 39, 46
  landscape, 89
  Laplantz, 123
  Mattar, 115
  May, 99
  Mazer, 59
  Mina, 100
  Shillito, 97
  silk, 112
  silver, 86, 112
  silver and marcasite, 52
  sixties, 75
  steel, 111
  Sterle, 55
  swordfish, 24
  thirties, 52
  Treen, 90
  Trifari, 70
  Van Cleef and Arpels, 47
  Weil, 78
  zoomorphic, 60
Bury, Claus, 112
Butler and Wilson, 90

C

Calder, Alexander, 58, 63
Cardin, Pierre, 79, 83
Cartier, house of, 7, 13, 34, 39, 40, 45, 55, 120
  bracelet, 46
  brooch, 46
  clock, 46
  icon, 90
  leopards, 57
  panthers, 57
  revival, 75
Cartier, Louis François, 39
chain:
  belt, 79
  silver, 35
Chanel, Coco, 40, 45, 68, 90
Chanel, Gabrielle, 48
Chang, Peter, 7
Charles, Geoffrey, 68
Chaumet, house of, 57
Chicago School of Design, 54
clasps, 14, 23
Clement, Jean, 47
clips, 21, 46
  steel and enamel, 57
  thirties, 36
Coates, Kevin, 121
cocktail style, 56
Colonna, Edward, 13
Constructivism, 85
consumer boom, 66
Cooper, John Paul, 14
Corocraft, 41, 68

Costin, Simon, 102
costume jewelry, 7, 40–50, 52, 62
  body cage, 106
  Chanel, 48
  consumer boom, 68
  eighties, 86
  fifties, 49
  mask, 106
  Pop Art motifs, 91
  seventies, 86
  sixties, 75, 83
  theatrical, 62
Costume Jewelry in Vogue, 34
Courrèges, 79
Cousens, Cynthia, 86
Crafts Council, 88, 94
  Jewelry Project, 88
  Jewelry Redefined, 88
Craftsman's Art, 88
Craftsman, The, 24
Cubism, 30, 33, 37
Cymric ware, 23

D

Dadaism, 45, 47
Dali, Salvador, 30, 31, 47, 58, 60
Darmstadt, 19
Dawson, Nelson, 16
decoration:
  botanical, 22, 104
  Celtic, 14, 16, 35
  curvilinear, 12, 16
  figurative, 57, 92, 121
  insect, 22
  kinetic, 124
  motifs, 37, 57, 63, 78, 89, 91
  organic, 78, 82, 99, 104
  primeval, 14
  rectilinear, 20
  Renaissance, 35
  sculptural, 92–3, 101, 104
  sentimental, 89
  spiritual, 121
  zigzag, 37, 63
Degen, Joel, 99
Degen, Pierre, 106
de Patta, Margaret, 60, 63
Depression, the, 45
Desprès, Jean, 34
Deutscher Werkbund, 19, 20
Dior, Christian, 62, 68
Donald, John, 80, 82, 91
Drescoll, 40
Dubuffet, 58
Dufrene, Maurice, 13
Dunand, Jean, 34
Dunlop, Sybil, 16–7, 34–5, 44
Du Pont co, 75

E

earrings, 17, 33
  anodized aluminium, 108
  arabesque, 60
  Coppola and Toppo, 49
  Dali, 47
  furry button, 68
  Har, 60
  hooped, 89
  krinos, 95
  plastic, 102
  polyester, 77
  Ramshaw, 83
  Trifari, 72
Ebendorf, Robert, 117
Egyptology, 29
Electrum, London, 94
Ellwood, Kim, 111
Ernst, Max, 47
ethnic revivals, 89
Exposition des Arts Decoratifs, 29

F

Faberge, 7
factory production, 8
Fahrner, Theodor, 19–20
fantasy jewelry, 82
femme fatale, 12, 13, 66
Feuillâtre, Eugène, 13

Findly, Anne, 77, 88
fine art jewelry, 58–61, 70, 72, 79
Fischer, Kate, 14
Flockinger, Gerda, 82
Follot, Paul, 13
Fontana, 58
forties, the, 51–62
Fouquet, Georges, 11, 13, 28, 30, 34
Francis, Carrie, 34
Fraser, Simon, 103
Friedell, Clemens, 24
Futurism, 30
futuristic jewelry, 79

G

Garrard, 120
Gaskin, Arthur and Georgina, 16, 23
German designers, 112
Giacometti, Alberto, 58
Gilbert, William, 103
Givenchy, 90
Glasgow School of Art, 16
Gralnick, Lisa, 125
Grima, Andrew, 75, 82
Gripoix, 40
Gropius, Walter, 54
Grosse Florein Co, 41
Guild of Handicraft, 15–6, 25
Guillard, Lucien, 13
Guimard, Hector, 12

H

Harper's Bazaar, 40
Harper, William, 92, 117
Hart, May, 16, 25
Hartwell, Josephine, 24
Haskell, Miriam, 41, 66, 67
hatpins, 14
Hebst, Marion, 112
Henkel, Heinrich, Co, 41
Heron, Susanna, 93, 101
Herz, 45
Hillier, Bevis, 30
Hoffman, Josef, 21
Hogg, Dorothy, 101
Horta, Victor, 12
Huber, Patriz, 19

I

iconography, 7, 16, 90
industrial production, 8, 53, 56, 80
  Far East, 54
  Hong Kong, 54
  US, 42
Industrial Revolution, 33
interior design, 12

J

Jamison, Nuala, 101
Japanese:
  black-enamel, 34
  design, 13
  exhibition, 88
  goods, 16, 43
  influence, 118
  market, 33
Jennings, Trevor, 118
Jensen, Georg, 21, 65, 73
Jensen, Soren George, 73
Jourdan, Charles, 83
Jugend magazine, 18
Jugendstijl, 19, 21
Jünger, Hermann, 82, 124
junk jewelry, 40, 75

K

King, Jessie, 14, 23
Klimt, Gustav, 12, 21
Knox, Archibald, 23
Koehler, Florence D, 24
Koppel, Henning, 65, 73
Kramer, Sam, 70
Krinos, Daphne, 94–5

Kruger, Daniel, 124
Kunzli, Otto, 124

L

La Belle Epoque, 13, 22
Lacloche, 27, 55
Lalique, René, 13–22, 75
La Maison de l'art Nouveau, 13
La Maison Moderne, 13
La Maison Vever, 13
Lane, Kenneth, 75
Laplantz, David, 122–3
Laurent, Yves Saint, 68
Lee Hu, Mary, 117
Leersum, Emmy Van, 79, 80, 112, 114, 122
Liberty and Co, 14, 16, 24
Liberty, Arthur Lasenby, 23

M

machine age, 34
Mackintosh, Charles Rennie, 16
Malinowski, 73
Manheim, Julia, 101, 106
Mann, Adrian, 68
Man Ray, 58
Marcus and Co, 24
Martinazzi, Bruno, 58
materials:
   acrylic, 36, 46, 54, 93, 125
   aluminium, 79, 86, 108, 114, 122
   amethyst, 24, 35
   Bakelite, 43, 45, 90
   black enamel, 34
   black onyx, 32
   black rubber, 80
   bone, 89
   bronze, 12
   casein, 43
   cellulose, 43
   ceramic, 23
   chrome, 33, 36, 43
   chyrophrase, 22–3
   citrine, 70
   cloissone, 16, 117
   color-core, 104
   copper, 24, 83
   coral, 32, 34
   cornelian, 45
   diamond, 13, 22, 45
   ebony, 125
   egg-crate plex, 122
   enamel, 14, 111
   gilded brass, 81, 104
   glass, 12, 23
      engraved, 13
      lava 18
      stained, 13, 18
   gold, 13, 22, 79, 80, 88, 106, 124
      enamels, 13, 117
      leaf, 111
   horn, 13, 16, 43
   ivory, 12, 43, 48, 89
   jade, 34, 45
   lizard skin, 122
   lucite, 46
   marcasite, 24, 36
   melamine, 54
   moon crystals, 24
   moonstone, 23, 35, 121
   mosaic, 24
   mother-of-pearl, 12, 115
   neon, 122
   neoprene, 104
   niobium, 96
   nylon, 54

olivine, 23
onyx, 24, 36
opals, 24, 35
paper, 83, 88, 104, 113
pearl, 13, 45
pebbles, 24
peridot, 23, 70
Perspex, 83, 84, 93, 99
plastic, 35, 42–46, 52, 60, 63, 89–91
platinum, 79
polystyrene, 54
polythene, 54
pvc (vinyl), 54, 113
rhinestone, 43
rubber, 91
shell, 16
silk, 79, 112
silver, 14, 34, 86, 112
stainless steel, 60, 63
steel, 104, 106, 111, 114
synthetic, 7, 43
tin, 40, 111
titanium, 79, 96, 97, 104
topaz, 35
tortoiseshell, 43
Mattar, Wilhelm, 115
Mawdsley, Richard, 92, 117
May, Susan, 99
Mazer, Jo, 59
media influence, 8
Meier-Graefe, Julius, 13
Metal Arts Guild, 63
Metcalf, Lynn, 88
Meyer Bros, 46
Mina, Jacqueline, 100
Miyake, Issey, 106
Moholy-Nagy, Lazlo, 54, 63
Morris, William, 8
motifs:
   Celtic, 14, 16
   floral, 16
   greyhound, 37
   Pop Art, 91
   pyramid, 37
   sunburst, 37
Mucha, Alphonse, 11, 13
Mulvagh, Jane, 34
Munson, Julia, 24
Murphy, H G, 42
Muthesius, Hermann, 19

N

Napier Inc, 41, 68
neckpiece, 9, 83
   Adam, 81
   aluminium, 79
   amethyst, 19
   Bakker, 113
   Dali, 47
   plastic, 88, 90
   silver, 42
   silver and amethyst, 19
   Torus 280 (B1), 8
   Trifari, 70, 72
   Watkins, 87, 98, 104

O

Olbrich, Josef Maria, 19, 21
organic jewelry, 78, 82, 86
Osman, Louis, 82
Ozbek, Rifat, 7, 91

P

Packard, Gillian, 75, 80, 82
pagan symbolism, 22
Paris International
   Exhibition, 13, 37, 47

Paris Metro, 12
Partridge, Fred, 16, 25
patriotic accessories, 40
Paul Flato, house of, 55
Paul, Iribe, 40
Pederson, Bent Gabrielson, 73
pendants, 13–5, 22, 25, 30
   acrylic, 104
   aluminium, 104
   gold, 110
   Hensel, 110
   ivory, 110
   landscape, 89
   Medusa, 92
   plastic, 35
   quartz crystal, 110
   silver gilt, 44
Pforzheim, 41, 52, 82
Picasso, Pablo, 30–1, 48, 58, 85
Poiret, Paul, 40
Pomodoro, Gio and Arnaldo, 58
Pop Art, 75, 78, 91
Poston, David, 96
precious gemstones, 7, 12, 23
precious metals, 7
Premet, 40
Punk movement, 91

Q

Quant, Mary, 75

R

Rabanne, Paco, 79
Ramsden, Omar, 16
Ramshaw, Wendy, 9, 82–5, 96, 99
Rational Dress Society, 23
Reiling, Reinhold, 82
Renaissance, the, 16, 68
   enamel work, 35
   reproductions, 75
Richilieu, 41
rings:
   Coates, 121
   Costin, 102
   Hogg, 101
   May, 99
   Pederson, 73
   Ramshaw, 83, 84, 85
   Treen, 89
Rothman, Gerd, 112
Royal College of Art, 8, 103
Ruskin, John, 8

S

Salon du Champs Mars
   gallery, 13
Sandoz, Gerard, 34
Sant'Angelo, Giorgio di, 75
Scandinavian folk art, 16, 21
   design, 73
   designers, 73
   influence, 95
Scheherezade, 39
Schiaparelli, Elsa, 40, 47–9, 82
Schlumberger, Jean, 58, 82
Schmuck International, 88
sculptural jewelry, 92–3, 101, 104, 106, 110, 116
   kinetic, 124
Sharlin, Miriam, 124
Shields, Jody, 66, 74, 83
Shillito, Ann Marie, 96–7
Silver, Rex, 23
sixties jewelry, 75–8
   British designers, 75
   ephemera, 83

flower power, 89–90
social history of jewelry, 7–9
Solvay Hotel, Brussels, 12
Spiller, Eric, 99
Stabler, Harold, 16
Studio Crafts, 80
Style of the Century, The, 30
suburban jewelry, 69
Succession group, 21
Surrealism, 45, 47, 51, 60
symbolism, 13
   pagan, 22
   scarab beetle, 29
Symbolist movement, 12

T

Tanguy, 58
techniques:
   casting, 13
   paper-making, 108
   plique-à-jour, 13, 16, 22
technology, 8, 22, 52, 104, 114
Templier, Raymond, 34, 37
thirties, the, 45–50
Thresher, Brainerd Bliss, 24
Tiffany and Co, 18, 24, 35, 82–3, 120
Tiffany, Louis Comfort, 18
Tiffany Studios, 24
Tilander, A, 53
torque, 101
Torus neckpiece, 8
Toussaint, Jean, 57
traditional jewelry, 7, 45
Traebert and Hoeffer, 55
Treen, Gunilla, 89–90
Trifari, Kraussman and Fishel, 41, 45, 54, 68–9, 70, 72
Tudric ware, 23
Tutenkhamun, 29
twenties, the, 39–45

U

utility design, 56

V

vacuum form, 7
Van Cleef and Arpels, 47, 55
Van der Velde, Henry, 19–21
Vedura, house of, 55
Vever, Henri and Paul, 13
Victoria and Albert museum, 88
Victoriana, 52
Vienna, Museum of Applied
   Arts, 21
Vogue magazine, 40–1, 94

W

Walter Scaife Ltd, 68
Watkins, David, 8, 82, 86–7, 98–9, 104–105
Watkins, Mildred, 24
Webb, David, 74
Wedgwood, 85
Weil, Georges, 24
Westwood, Vivienne, 91
Whitby jet, 52
Wiener Werkstätte, 20, 21
Wiening, Henette, 112
Wilson, Henry, 16
Windsor, Duchess of, 57
Woolf, Lam de, 116
wrist-watch, 34, 91
Wynne, Madeline, 24

CREDITS

p6 Susan Barr; p7 Peter Chang; p8 David Watkins; p9 Wendy Ramshaw; p10 c Christies; p12 Bridgman Art Library; p13 John Jesse & Irina Laski; p14 John Jesse & Irina Laski; p15 John Jesse & Irina Laski; p16 John Jesse & Irina Laski; p17 Angelo Hornak Library; p18 E.T. Archive; p19 top John Jesse & Irina Laski; bottom Tadema Gallery, Camden Passage, London; p20 Tadema Gallery, Camden Passage, London; p21 all Tadema Gallery, Camden Passage, London; p22 c SPADEM 1985; p23 Tadema Gallery, Camden Passage, London; p24 Silver, London; p25 John Jesse & Irina Laski; p27 Angelo Hornak Library; p28 top Angelo Hornak Library; bottom John Jesse & Irina Laski; p29 all Angelo Hornak Library; p30 all c Christies; p31 John Jesse & Irina Laski; p32 c Christies; p33 all Angelo Hornak Library; p34 top John Jese & Irina Laski; bottom E.T. Archive; p35 John Jesse & Irina Laski; p36 Angelo Hornak Library; p37 c Christies; p38 John Jesse & Irina Laski; p40 c Christies; p41 John Jesse & Irina Laski; p42 Tadema Gallery, Camden Passage, London; p43 Angelo Hornak Library; p44 John Jesse & Irina Laski; p45 c Christies; p46 c Christies; p47 c Christies; p48 Maria Merola; p49 Maria Merola; p50 John Jesse & Irina Laski; p52 Maria Merola; p53 top John Jesse & Irina Laski; bottom c Christies; p54 right c Christies; left Maria Merola; p55 all John Jesse & Irina Laski; p56 top John Jesse & Irina Laski; bottom John Jesse & Irina Laski; p57 all John Jesse & Irina Laski; p58 top Bruno Martinazzi; bottom c Christies; p59 Maria Merola; p60 Maria Merola; p61 Tadema Gallery, Camden Passage, London; p62 John Jesse & Irina Laski; p63 Collection FIFTY-50, New York; p64 Tadema Gallery, Camden Passage, London; p66 Maria Merola; p67 Maria Merola; p68 Maria Merola; p69 Maria Merola; p70 top Collection FIFTY-50, New York; bottom Maria Merola; p71 Maria Merola; p72 Maria Merola; p73 Tadema Gallery, Camden Passage, London; p74 c Christies; p75 all Tadema Gallery, Camden Passage, London; p76 Anne Finlay; p78 Tadema Gallery, Camden Passage, London; p79 Gijs Bakker Design; p80 Tadema Gallery, Camden Passage, London; p81 Gijs Bakker Design; p82 Wendy Ramshaw; p83 Wendy Ramshaw; p84 all Wendy Ramshaw; p85 all Wendy Ramshaw; p86 Cynthia Cousens; p87 all David Watkins; p88 top Anne Finlay; bottom Lynn Metcalf; p89 all Gunilla Treen; p90 all Gunilla Treen; p91 Tadema Gallery, Camden Passage, London; p92 Richard Mawdsley; p93 Susanna Heron/photo David Ward; p94 Daphne Krinos; p95 Daphne Krinos; p96 all Ann-Marie Shillito; p97 Ann-Marie Shillito; p98 David Watkins; p99 all Susan May; p100 Jacqueline Mina; p101 left Dorothy Hogg; right Malcolm Appleby; p102 Simon Fraser; p103 William Gilbert; p104 all David Watkins; p105 David Watkins; p106 Julia Manheim; p107 Julia Manheim; p108 Jane Adam; p109 Jane Adam; p110 all David Hensel; p111 Kim Ellwood; p112 Galerie Ra, Amsterdam; p113 Gijs Bakker Design; p114 Gijs Bakker Design; p115 Wilhelm Mattar; p116 Lam de Woolf/Galerie Ra, Amsterdam; p117 William Harper; p118 all Trevor Jennings; p119 David Hensel; p120 Susan Barr; p121 Kevin Coates; p122 all David Laplantz; p123 David Laplantz; p125 all Lisa Gralnick. Quintet would also like to thank Helen Craven and Dierdrie O'Day for their help with this publication.